D0875610

Ethnic Alienation
The Italian-Americans

Ethnic Alienation
The Italian-Americans

Patrick J. Gallo

Rutherford • Madison • Teaneck
Fairleigh Dickinson University Press

© 1974 by Associated University Presses, Inc.
Associated University Presses, Inc.
Cranbury, New Jersey 08512

Library of Congress Cataloging in Publication Data

Gallo, Patrick J
    Ethnic alienation.

    Bibliography: p.
    1. Italians in the United States. I. Title.
E184.I8G34   301.45'15'1073   72-9915
ISBN 0-8386-1244-X

to
Grace

Contents

Preface

That this book has at last come to fruition is owing to the guidance, assistance, and moral encouragement of many fine people. I hope that this modest attempt to acknowledge their efforts on my behalf will in some measure convey to them my deep gratitude and affection.

I am particularly indebted to Professor I. William Zartman, Chairman, Department of Politics, New York University, for his always generous and able guidance. An exceptional scholar and teacher, his compassion, patience, and gentle encouragement have made him a truly inspirational figure to me.

Professor Kalman Silvert, New York University, helped to introduce me to the excitement of field work and theory. He especially guided me in the theoretical and methodological aspects of this study, giving freely of his time and many talents. Professor Rita Cooley, New York University, made useful suggestions on many sections, as did Professor Gino Germani, Harvard University, with valuable insights in Chapter 3 in particular.

Special recognition must be accorded Mr. Joseph Follayttar, head librarian, Teaneck High School, who gave indispensable aid at all stages, particularly when the formulation of the work was in its infancy.

I thank Mr. Joseph Zimmitti for his assistance in the translation of the interview schedule into Italian, and also extend my gratitude to all who helped in the various operational phases: Dr. Leonard Covello, Father Michael Castrelli, Mr. Salvatore Scotto, Mr. Vito Pietenza, and Mr. Michael Pesce. Miss Annette Bruno provided a wide variety of help without hesitation. I shall always be grateful. I owe a special debt to Mrs. Mathilde E. Finch, Editor, Fairleigh Dickinson University Press, for her generous and wise counsel.

And special thanks go to my interviewees. I was fortunate in having respondents who were cooperative, warm, and gracious. This book would scarcely have been possible without them! I shall always remember them with fond affection.

Although they were not involved in the design or formulation of this study, I would like to mention here Professor Philip Cohen, Montclair State College, and Professor Richard N. Swift, New York University, both of whom have had a profound effect upon me.

I shall be eternally grateful to Mr. and Mrs. Andrew Bruno for their love and prayers. Their undying support and encouragement have sustained their son-in-law through the completion of this book.

Last, but not least in importance, I thank my wife, Grace. This volume literally would not have been possible without her many different kinds of help, especially in the formulation and translation of the interview schedule as well as in other aspects. Her patience, encouragement, sacrifice, and loving thoughtfulness are without limit. Perhaps the best way of letting her know my gratitude and love is to dedicate this book to her.

To Laura Ann and Andrew, our beautiful children, I must express an apology. They often had to heed the all-too-familiar injunction, "Shh!" Their presence and love helped to keep their daddy on an even keel at the stormiest of times.

I alone must bear full responsibility for whatever short-comings there are in this study.

P. J. G.

Acknowledgments

I would like to thank the following authors and publishers for permission to reprint various selections in this book:

Atheneum Publishers for permission to quote copyrighted material excerpted from *The Italians* by Luigi Barzini. Copyright © 1964 by Luigi Barzini. Reprinted by permission of Atheneum Publishers.

Leonard Covello for permission to quote from *The Social Background of the Italo-American School Child,* published by E. J. Brill, 1967.

S. N. Eisenstadt for permission to quote from *The Absorption of Immigrants,* published by Routledge & Kegan Paul Ltd, 1954.

Oxford University Press for permission to quote from *Assimilation in American Life,* 1963.

Introduction

In his news conference following a stunning defeat in the New York mayoral primary, the incumbent, John Lindsay, attributed the causes for this turn of events to "built-in bigotry . . . reaction . . . fear . . . backlash."[1] A number of people continued to interpret the campaign as one in which the forces of oppression and backlash opposed those of reconciliation and human progress. The designated representatives of the backlash sentiment were Mario Proccacino (D) and State Senator John J. Marchi (R). Moreover, both Proccacino and Marchi were of Italian descent, and had received the heavy endorsement of the Italian-American community in the primary and the November election.[2] This served to solidify the "backlash" interpretation of the election in general and Italian-American political behavior in particular. According to this interpretation the Italian-American is a conservative, and in this instance a right-wing extremist whose alienation was expressing itself in appeals to law and order, and an anti-black posture. James Breslin,

1. *New York Times*, June 1, 1969, p. 1.
2. According to the WCBS-TV news estimate in sample districts which were predominantly Italian-American, Lindsay received 15% of the vote, Proccacino 55%, and Marchi 30% (November, 1969).

15

a candidate in the primary, seemed to advance this interpretation in an article describing the mood of black revolution in Cleveland. Reporting on a planned police ambush, and the police's overreaction to it, he concludes,

> and on Mayfield Road, a quarter of a mile from the East Side the Italians stood on street corners and talked about George Wallace. "He knows what to do, and so do we," a man standing in front of Presti's bakery was saying, "all I know is that you could go into a very good business today. Selling M-1's."[3]

This study will investigate these assumptions, since little evidence has appeared to support the interpretation that was current during the campaign of 1969.

The data that form the core of this study were gathered by in-depth interviews of three groups, a total of forty-five men and women.[4] The first group was composed of fifteen southern Italians who recently migrated to the United States and who now live in the New York metropolitan region.[5] The second group consisted of a total of fifteen respondents, five first, second, and third generation Italian-Americans whose families originated in southern Italy.[6] The primary reason for selecting a three generational span is to explain generational differences and similarities. The third group was composed of fifteen white Anglo-Saxon Protestants. The latter served as a control group.

---

3. Although Mr. Breslin's article appeared a year before the primary, it does capture the interpretation that was widespread prior to and during the campaign. *New York Post*, July 25, 1958, pp. 1, 31.

4. Herbert Hyman, *Interviewing in Social Research* (Chicago: University of Chicago Press, 1954). See also Robert Kahn and Charles Cannell, *The Dynamics of Interviewing* (New York: John Wiley, 1957).

5. I shall refer to this group as Italian immigrants.

6. I shall refer to the first-, second-, and third-generation respondents collectively as Italian-Americans. Separately, I will designate them as: first-generation, second-generation, and third-generation, Italian-Americans. By first-generation Italian-Americans I mean those residents in the U.S. who were born in Italy and now are citizens. Second-generation Italian-Americans are those who are native-born of Italian parentage. I shall refer to the third generation as those respondents born in the United States of native-born parents. I will refer to all groups collectively as Italians.

No pretense is made by the author that thirty cases is a representative cross section of the entire Italian-American universe. However, while acknowledging this limitation, it should not lead to an opposite conclusion that these thirty cases are isolated individuals in that universe.

As its focus this study will try to determine whether the American political system tends to neutralize or sharpen an ethnic group's sense of exclusion from the dominant roles, values, and institutions, and result in types of behavior that differentiate them from native whites. It will, therefore, shed some light on whether the American political system tends toward the integration or exclusion of some ethnic groups. Political alienation will be operationally defined as the rejection by the individual of the dominant political roles, values, and institutions of society based upon the real or imagined exclusion of the individual from the political processes of society by other individuals or groups.

For many years the perceptions of political life held by those within a given political system have been of great concern to political scientists. A number of them contend that citizen support plays a major role in determining the structure and processes of political systems.[7] David Easton affirms the fundamental importance of attitudes for system stability by centering on "diffuse support as a prerequisite for the integration of political systems. He contends that where the input drops below a certain level the "persistence of any kind of system will be endangered. A system will finally succumb unless it adopts measures to cope with the stress."[8]

This study will attempt to deal with a number of dimensions of an individual's perception of political life.[9] The

---

7. Gabriel Almond and Sidney Verba, *"The Civic Culture"* (Princeton, N.J.: Princeton University Press, 1963) .

8. David Easton, *A Systems Analysis of Political Life* (New York: John Wiley, 1965) , p. 220.

9. Charles Backstrom and Gerald Marsh, *Survey Research* (Chigao, Ill.: Northwestern University Press, 1963) . See also: Morris Hansen, W. M. Hurwitz and W. G. Madow, *Sample Survey Methods and Theory* (New York: John Wiley, 1953) .

interviews of Italian immigrants will tell us what they bring to their new environment. What are their perceptions of Italian politics? What factors influence those perceptions? What are their predispositions? Do their political perceptions indicate that they are politically alienated before they arrive in the United States? The data gathered by interviewing the second group of first-, second-, and third-generation Italian-Americans will determine the impact of the American political system upon the perceptions of the new arrival, and the intergenerational changes in them. What is the Italian-American's image of himself? Does the self-image conform to the one held by others in the community or the broader society? Do the perceptions of political life held by Italian-Americans indicate that they are politically alienated? To what extent are their perceptions governed by the real or imagined exclusions from the dominant roles and institutions of society? Do their subjective feelings conform to the objective "realities"? What role do assimilation, ethnicity, class, and religion play in their perceptions of political life?

In spite of increasing assimilation, why does ethnicity still play an important role in the political behavior of various ethnic groups? Robert Dahl contends that ". . . in spite of growing assimilation, ethnic factors continued to make themselves felt with astonishing tenacity," but despite this, he continues, "the strength of ethnic ties as a factor in local politics must surely recede."[10] Raymond Wolfinger observes that ethnic voting patterns persist into the second and third generations and that "at least in New Haven, all the social changes of the 1940s and 1950s do not seem to have reduced the political importance of national origins."[11] Michael Pa-

---

10. Robert Dahl, *Who Governs?* (New Haven, Conn.: Yale University Press, 1961) , p. 59.

11. Raymond Wolfinger, "The Development and Persistence of Ethnic Voting," *American Political Science Review* (December 1965) , pp. 896–908. Hereinafter cited as APSR. See also Raymond Wolfinger "Some Consequences of Ethnic Politics," in M. Kent Jennings and Harmon Zeigler, *The Electoral Process* (Englewood Cliffs, N.J.: Prentice Hall, 1961) , pp. 42–54.

renti asserts that Dahl and Wolfinger were asking the wrong question in their approach since a conceptual distinction between acculturation and assimilation had not been made. He concludes, "The disappearance of ethnicity as a factor in political behavior waits in large part upon the total ethnic structural identificational assimilation into the host society . . . before relegating them to the history of tomorrow, the unassimilated ethnics should be seen as very much alive and with us today."[12] The added importance of this study is that it will attempt to clarify the salience of ethnicity in the political perceptions of Italian-Americans, and the politically relevant choices they make.[13]

Descriptive Model

The attempt to expain the interaction between perception and behavior leads inevitably to a search for the relationships between variables. The study of the perceptions of political life held by an ethnic group will be based on a prior model.

A particular response by an individual is channeled by certain predispositions and follows some external occurrence perceived as a stimulus. Put another way, response may be viewed as a function of the interaction between stimuli coming from the environment and the particular predispositions possessed by the individual at a given point in time. Since the individual may be bombarded by stimuli from all sides, he must perceive selectively. Thus, the individual develops a perceptual screen, which filters some stimuli and eliminates others. A mutual reinforcement follows upon the in-

---

12. Michael Parenti, "Ethnic Politics and the Persistence of Ethnic Identification," *APSR* (September 1967), p. 726. My findings support Parenti's conclusion.

13. Michael Parenti, *Ethnic and Political Attitudes: Three Generations of Italian Americans* (Ph.D. dissertation, Yale University, 1962). See also Gustave Serino, "Italians in the Political Life of Boston: A Study of an Immigrant and Ethnic Group in the Political Life of an Urban Community" (Ph.D. dissertation, Harvard University, 1950), and Gideon Sjoberg and Roger Nett, "Cultural and Social Strictures in Social Research," *A Methodology for Social Research* (New York: Harper & Row, 1968), pp. 112–20.

teraction among stimuli, predispositions, and responses to produce patterns of behavior.[14] One source of stimulus is group membership such as a family, religion, social class, and ethnic group. In addition, the social and political institutions of the United States are important stimuli, along with neighborhood residence and community indentification.

Ethnic enclaves are formed by the interaction between a certain set of stimuli and predispositions. Earlier residential patterns and family-linked immigration are major factors in the urban concentration of an ethnic group. An urban concentration is reinforced if the immigration of an ethnic group is part of the rural-to-urban flow underway in the country of origin. The numerical size of an ethnic group and its urban concentration contribute to the formation of the ethnic enclave. The ethnic enclave is formed as a result of another kind of stimulus, namely, outgroup rejection.[15] The need for psychoogical satisfaction and security are particular predispositions possessed by the ethnic. These predispositions are reinforced by living with fellow ethnics, making it possible for the rejected to move with confidence toward interaction with the larger society. Ethnic residential patterns change as a result of movement into the higher socioeconomic categories, along with outgroup acceptance, and assimilation.

Familism, which emerges out of the social structure of an ethnic's country of origin, is internalized in the individual personality. Familism leads to an inability on the part of some ethnic groups to form any kind of meaningful association outside the nuclear family. Familism as a predisposition is brought with the ethnic when he immigrates.

---

14. Portions of this model are adapted from those developed by Robert Lane and Lester Milbrath. Robert Lane, *Political Life* (New York: The Free Press, 1959). Lester Milbrath, *Political Participation* (Chicago: Rand McNally & Co., 1965).

15. Robin Williams, Jr., *Strangers Next Door* (Englewood Cliffs, N. J.: Prentice Hall, 1964), pp. 17–27.

This predisposition, subject to the stimulus of urban living, is gradually altered. An ethnic group that migrates to an urban environment from an essentially rural area tends to undergo a series of changes in its family structure. More specifically, the length of urban residence by a rural ethnic group and its intergenerational mobility is related to less immediate family participation, fewer extended family relationships, and greater extrafamilial social relations. No longer will the family be the center of each member's life. The decision-making in the family will tend to shift from father-dominated to a shared role by the third generation. The ethnic family will be less oriented toward inherited traditions. This changed orientation will have a bearing on a changed political outlook, particularly in the formation of notions of the public good, of obligation to community, and of increased personal trust. As a consequence, the ethnic will more likely form corporate groups that link family with the larger society.

From the social and political institutions of the United States flow other stimuli. The institutionalization of an ethnic's behavior occurs within the social structure.[16] Subsequent assimilation proceeds on several levels: cultural, structural, marital, identificational, attitude receptional, behavior receptional, and civic.[17] Cultural assimilation or acculturation refers to the adoption of the basic values and patterns of behavior of the host society. Structural assimilation involves the complete acceptance of ethnics into the primary face-to-face relationships by the members of the host society. Acculturation may occur without structural assimilation. Once structural assimilation takes place, with or subsequent to acculturation, all of the other types of assimi-

---

16. I adopt here the definition by Gordon, which views social structure as "a set of crystallized social relationships which members have with each other which places them in groups . . . and which relates them to the major institutional activities of the society." Milton Gordon, *Assimilation in American Life* (New York: Oxford University Press, 1964), pp. 30–31.

17. I will discuss the interrelationships of these levels in chapter 3.

lation will follow. An ethnic group's lack of structural assimilation will be evident in the kinds of demands made upon it by the core society. The lack of structural assimilation will result in a greater occupational, educational, and residential differentiation from native whites.

Though an ethnic may assimilate on a number of levels, he may not be structurally assimilated. The absence of a structural assimilation results in the retention of a distinct social identity. The active reality that is the ethnic community is the ethnic's subsociety, bound by a network of relationships that permit him to remain within its confines for most of their primary and some of his secondary relationships.[18] The ethnic subsociety is created by the intersection of the vertical stratifications of ethnicity with the horizontal stratifications of social class that we call *ethniclass*.[19] We view American society as a "mosaic" of ethnic groups based on race, religion, and national origins, interlaced by social class stratification. Residential patterns may change as a result of movement into higher socioeconomic categories. This does not result in the destruction of the ethnic subsociety, because a lack of structural assimilation reinforces the subsociety's existence. In addition, an ethnic subsociety is perpetuated despite the growing loss of an ecological base by the movement to the suburbs and by an increased affluence. When a person in a specific ethniclass moves, he takes his place within the same segment of the population segmented by ethnic group and social class. This situation is internalized, creating within the ethnic a perception of a series of subcommunities like his own.

We may also consider additional responses to the stimuli emanating from the social and political institutions of the

---

18. By primary relationships I mean those that are personal, intimate, emotionally affective, and those which bring into play the whole personality. Secondary relationships are impersonal, formal, and segmented, and tend not to come very close to the core of personality.

19. I have used Gordon's term *ethclass*, but changed it to *ethniclass* in order to make pronunciation easier.

United States. A structural separation has a direct relationship to feelings of political powerlessness and perceived political normlessness. As one moves from the first to the third generation, and from the lower to the higher occupational, income, and residential hierarchies, there is among ethnics a decreasing sense of powerlessness. An increase in perceived political normlessness becomes evident among the ethnics of the third generation since birth-in-America tends to be associated with lower levels of powerlessness, higher educational attainment, and a relative increase in the higher occupational and residential hierarchies. The movement into the higher occupational, income, and residential hierarchies does not mean that a structural fusion has taken place, but rather reflects a general condition of the American economy and the supports that a subsocietal identification provides. A changed family structure along the lines of an urban and democratic one is instrumental in a declining sense of powerlessness.

Political alienation as a response to the stimuli from the social and political institutions of the United States is associated with lower socioeconomic status. A low position in the social structure as determined by occupation, income, and education results in the inaccessibility to the means to achieve desired ends.

Political alienation among ethnics will be associated with certain responses such as low levels of interest and political participation, particularly in the following areas: political activity, political discussions, and organizational memberships. Party identification, however, may not have any independent relationship to low political alienation. Strict Catholics will tend to be associated with an overall reduction of political alienation while marginal Catholics are associated with political normlessnes.

While there is a relative increase in political interest and political activity across a three-generational span, political alienation among ethnics generally results in political withdrawal. However, appeals to the alienated based on fulfilling the need for political power, or ethnic appeals based on the politics of recognition, may stir the ethnics into greater political activity. Political powerlessness and political normlessness may interact significantly in a populist candidate. The results can be negative, but they more often may be positive defenses of acculturated values that the ethnic perceives as being threatened.

Selection of Respondents

The small number of cases was decided upon for a variety of reasons.[20] First, this form of interview could permit the probing in-depth of personal, societal, and attitudinal factors influencing an ethnic's perceptions of political life. It is comprehensive and pays greater attention to detail. The political scientist at the start of his research has to determine if he is going to paint in broad brush strokes a portrait of his subject or take a snapshot of political reality. The in-depth interview provides a close-up view of the individual and his personal life style, since the majority of the respondents were interviewed at home. Second, the in-depth interview makes it possible to uncover what a quantitative study may have missed or treated superficially and does not show in statistical tabulations. Third, the method is well suited to the Italian temperament in that it lends itself to informality. It particularly would reveal data on a personal level.

All this is not to say that there are no hazards or limitations in this approach. One of the major shortcomings is that the data may provide only generalizations on a few cases and may be taken only as hypotheses. An attempt will be made to balance this weakness by the use of supporting studies from different disciplines, many of which provide quantitative data and will help to describe the wider societal

20. Hansen *et al.*

matrix of the respondents' political perceptions. A second major shortcoming is that the abundance of material may defy classification and make it difficult to reach meaningful conclusions. The use of the control group will help to offset this weakness since differences, especially on the basis of national origin, social class, and religion will be made clearer.

Census and Immigration Bureau reports issued by both the American and Italian governments were used to ascertain immigration patterns and demographic characteristics. Based on this information, a determination was made of the areas from which the respondents would be selected.

Americans of Italian descent accounted for the largest wave of immigration in the history of the United States. Of the 2,300,000 Italian immigrants to the United States between 1899 and 1910, nearly two million were southern Italians. The crest of the immigrant wave was between 1901 and 1914, when the annual average of Italian immigrants totaled 616,000. About 90% of the Italian-Americans today have their origins in South Italy, and that same percentage trace their families to those who came between 1894 and 1914. Americans of Italian descent make up more than one sixth of the New York City population. Ninety percent live in urban areas and about 95% are Catholic. Italian immigration still tends to occur in families. The immigrant makes his first residence in communities whose population came from the same region, province, or even village.

Potential respondents among the new arrivals and Italian-Americans were selected according to the following criteria: socioeconomic status, age, sex, length of residence in the United States, generational status, and the section of Italy from which they originated. The author's community contacts supplied lists of potential respondents who met these criteria. Personal introductions were one form of contact. In other cases the potential respondent was approached by an intermediary who gave a brief explanation of the project.

He was then contacted by phone and given a more precise explanation of the study. The list of potential respondents was further refined following these initial contacts in an effort to arrive at a representative cross section. Respondents among Italian immigrants and Italian-Americans came from Paterson, New Jersey, and Brooklyn, New York. In Paterson over half of the population is of Italian descent.[21] Over one third of the foreign-born population in Paterson is Italian. Of the foreign-born Italians in New York City about 26% reside in Brooklyn.[22] There are no statistics for the precise number of immigrants who come to Brooklyn annually, but every source I approached made a subjective evaluation and concluded that the borough absorbed a very large number of the Italian immigrants.

Nine of the Italian immigrants were interviewed in their homes. An immigration center was used to meet the six others. Only three of the fifteen immigrants were contacted by phone; the rest came through personal introductions. The immigration center had a social hall where the Italian immigrants diverted themselves with card playing, lively conversation, bocce (an Italian game of bowls), or a cup of espresso. The author made the acquaintance of a few of the immigrants upon an introduction by the director of the center, who explained the purpose of my presence. Other introductions followed quite naturally when aroused curiosities tried to ascertain who the stranger was in their midst. A four-month period of observation took place, during which I took part in the activities and informal conversations.[23] This period was invaluable in yielding personal insights into individual and group behavior. Often I was able to detect contradictory information supplied by a particular

---

21. U. S. Census of Population, 1960, Part 24, Vol. 1 (Table 79). This includes first, second, and third generations.

22. Ninth Annual Statistical Guide for New York City, Department of Commerce and Industrial Development (1965), pp. 33–35.

23. S. M. Miller, "The Participant Observer and Overt Rapport," *American Sociological Review* (August 1952), pp. 97–99 (hereinafter cited as *ASR*). See also Sjoberg and Nett, "Direct Observation," pp. 160–87.

respondent in such informal conversations. I was warmly introduced as a friend or proudly as "Professore."

Of the fifteen Italian-American respondents, ten were interviewed in their homes and contacted by phone. The remaining five were interviewed at other locations, and that same number accounted for personal introductions.

Ministers of Episcopal churches in two separate communities not far from Paterson supplied a list of respondents who comprised the control group, according to the criteria previously employed. All fifteen of them were then contacted by phone and interviewed in their homes.

The respondents in all three groups were given a sufficient explanation about the nature of the study and the interview.[24] The data were recorded by simultaneous note-taking or by the use of a tape recorder. The use of one method of recording the data rather than the other was determined by the circumstances of the interview and the respondent's attitude. The Italian immigrants were not inhibited in the least by the presence of the tape recorder and, in fact, its presence lent additional significance to the study and the respondent's role in it. The interviews varied in length from one to three and one-half hours in single and split sessions.

The interview schedule was divided into twelve sections: I. Personal-Residence; II. Education; III. Family; IV. Religion; V. Work, Satisfaction, Income; VI. Class Identification; VII. Trust-Friendship; VIII. Acculturation, Assimilation, Ethnicity; IX. Ideology and Issues; X. Political Discussion and Information; XI. Political Efficacy; XII. Organization Membership-Political Party. Portions of the interview schedule employed by Robert Lane, Irwin Child, Michael Parenti, Gabriel Almond and Sidney Verba, and Leo Srole were adapted to this study.[25] The questions in the

24. Sjoberg and Nett, "The Ethics of Project Selection," p. 120.

25. Robert Lane, *Political Ideology* (New York: The Free Press, 1962) ; Irwin Child, *Italians or Americans* (New Haven: Yale University Press, 1943) ; Michael Parenti, *Ethnic and Political Attitudes;* Almond and Verba, *The Civic Culture;* C. R. Miller and E. W. Butler, "Anomia & Euomia: A

interview schedule were of an open ended variety which made them subject to secondary probes and guidance by the interviewer.[26]

The open-ended form of questions has certain advantages and disadvantages. The open-ended question encourages the respondent to structure those responses which have meaning to him. The topics chosen, the flow of thought, and even the expression of a response are telling aspects of a respondent's attitude and motivation.[27] There is some risk attached to this kind of question. Perhaps for some reason the respondent may lie, or exaggerate, or his memory may have failed him.[28] The scope and overlapping nature of the interview schedule served as one safeguard. The informal conversations that followed the interview served as another check. A brief review of the relevant literature will place this study in a wider context.

Related Studies

The literature dealing with alienation has centered around three interrelated questions: From whom or what is the individual alienated? What are the causes of alienation? In what forms of behavior is alienation manifested?

In some portions of the literature the focus is on the individual rather than societal conditions. "Alienation denotes an estrangement or separation," according to one researcher, "between parts of the whole personality and significant aspects of world experience. The sense, or feeling of the individual's estrangement is combined with the loss of identity

Methodological Evaluation of Srole's Anomia Scale," *ASR* (June 1966), pp. 400–406.

26. Lauren Wispe and Paul Thayer, "Some Methodological Problems in the Analysis of the Unstructured Interview," *Public Opinion Quarterly* (1954), pp. 223–27. (Hereinafter cited as *POQ*.)

27. Leo Crespi, "The Cheater Problem in Polling," *POQ* (1945), pp. 431–45.

28. Sjoberg and Nett, "The Structured Interview," pp. 193–202, and "The Unstructured Interview," pp. 211–23. See also Franklin Evans, "On Interview Cheating." *POQ* (Spring 1961), pp. 405–10.

or authentic being and depersonalization."[29] The individual's estrangement may involve an objective state of estrangement or separation, the subjective state of feeling of estranged personality, or a motivational state tending toward estrangement. Separation may, on the other hand, be between the self and the objective world or the self and aspects of the self. Keniston sees alienated people as "those who reject what they see as the dominant values, roles and institutions of their society."[30] This is crystallized to mean a conflict between roles given to an individual's own value orientation. He suggests that the term requires further specification in the following ways: Focus: Alienated from what? Replacement: What replaces the old relationships? Mode: How is alienation manifest? Agent: What is the agent of alienation?[31] Keniston has also suggested that "alienation, once seen as the consequence of a cruel (but changeable) economic order, has become for many the central fact of human existence, characterizing man's 'thrownness' into a world in which he has no inherent place. Formerly imposed upon men by the world around them, estrangement increasingly is chosen by them as their dominant reaction to the world."[32]

A second reference in the literature is decidedly Marxian, in that the emphasis is on the separation between the individual and the meaning of his work. Hegel used *alienation* as a description of what happens to socialized man. He becomes detached from the world of nature by his own nature. Marx saw labor as an alienating factor. The division of labor caused conflict between the interest of the single individual and the common interests of all individuals.[33] Daniel

29. Maurice Natanson, "Alienation and Social Role," *Social Research* (Autumn 1966) .

30. Kenneth Keniston, *The Uncommitted: Alienated Youth in American Society* (New York: Harcourt, Brace & World, Inc., 1956) , p. 454.

31. *Ibid.*

32. Kenneth Keniston, "Alienation and the Decline of Utopia," *American Scholar* (Spring 1960) , pp. 161–200.

33. Robert Nisbet, *The Sociological Tradition* (New York: Basic Books, 1966) , pp. 266–73.

Bell introduced the term "reification" a "philosophical category with psychological overtones" as opposed to estrangement, a socio-psychological condition. Bell uses the term to
describe Marx's concept of alienation as "dehumanization"
of individuals under exploitative social conditions, in contrast to the current view of alienation as denoting attitudes
of estrangement.[34] Reification involves a judgment about the
quality of human life in a particular social setting. Estrangement on the other hand is a subjective attitude about the
social life that is held by the participant individuals themselves. The former is measured against objective standards,
the latter is determined by studying attitudes of individuals.[35]

Alienation is also seen in a third manner, namely, as a
sense of historical dislocation in which society's goals and
the meaning of community are abortive.[36]

The literature on alienation suggests the lack of clarity
given to the concept. It is often used as a catchall for many
related and unrelated concepts. On the one hand, it is used
to describe an objective sociological phenomenon, i.e., the
socially caused role of conflict separating man from man.
On the other hand, it describes a subjective psychological
phenomenon, namely, the thoughts and feelings resulting
from this separation. One word is used to describe both a
sociological fact and the psychological reflection,[37] hence
the effort by Bell, Aberach, and others to clarify the term.
"A person must naturally wonder if it might not simply be
better to discard the term," writes Keniston. However, he is
certain, "that the same problem of definition would crop
up again and again with some cognate term like estrange-

---

34. Daniel Bell, "The Rediscovery of Alienation: Some Notes Along the
Quest for the Historical Marx," *Journal of Philosophy* 56 (1959) : 933–34.
35. *Ibid.*
36. Herbert Stroup, "A Historical Explanation of Alienation," *Social Casework* (March 1961) , pp. 107–11.
37. Helen Lamb and N. S. Lehrman, "On Alienation: Two Contrasting
Views," *Science and Society* (Summer 1961) , pp. 260–69.

ment, disaffection, or detachment."[38] Joel Aberbach argues for the retention of the term because "it has been employed in a great number of widely used theories and one task of scholars at this point should be to clarify when and how various forms of alienation do serve as important independent or intervening variables and whether these attitudes are meaningfully structured in people's minds."[39]

Causes and Manifestations of Alienation

Melvin Seeman isolates five basic ways in which the concept of alienation has been used in the literature. His typology includes powerlessness, meaninglessness, normlessness, isolation, and self-estrangement. He suggests that an effort be made to explore the interrelationship between operational measures of these variants in addition to the causes and consequences of them.[40] I will use this typology as the framework for the remainder of this review.

The concept of anomie first appeared in 1893 in a book by Emile Durkheim. In it he associated the idea of anomie with that of the division of labor. He tried to account for the "pathological" forms and consequences of labor by pointing to the "imperfect coordination" of the parts, the decline of social solidarity, and conflict among the social classes.[41] The division of labor did not permit enough interaction to permit the development of a set of common rules. In the absence of the rules, confusion and unpredictability were magnified.[42]

---

38. *The Uncommitted*, p. 454.

39. Joel Aberbach, "Alienation and Political Behavior," *APSR* (March 1969), p. 87.

40. Melvin Seeman, "On the Meaning of Alienation," *ASR* (December 1959), pp. 783–91.

41. Sebastian de Grazia, *The Political Community* (Chicago: University of Chicago Press, 1948), pp. 3–6. See also: Kaspur Naegle, "Attachment and Alienation: Complementary Aspects of the Work of Durkheim and Simmel," *American Journal of Sociology* (May 1958), pp. 580–89. (Hereinafter cited as *AJS*.)

42. de Grazia, p. 5.

In other works Durkheim related anomie to certain social phenomena like suicide and to certain economic phenomena like variations in the business cycle. In *Le Suicide* he pointed to the fact that the suicide rate increased at about the same rate in both economic crisis and prosperity. This factor explains anomie. When no body of common values and sentiments exists, a person then feels isolated and lost, without any norms to guide him. He is certain neither of his place nor of his role in society. A sense of confusion and loss of orientation results when expectations are frustrated in depression and satiated in unusual prosperity. Durkheim meant to use *anomie* to describe the "disintegrated state of a society that possesses no body of common values or morals which effectively govern conduct. He therefore described anomie as a condition of relative normlessness within a society that occurs as traditional moral norms are weakened or destroyed."[43] Although anomie in society might produce alienation within individuals, a person could feel alienated from a social system with strong normative integration. Hence, anomie as a characteristic of societies or other organizations cannot be equated with individual alienation.

Others have upheld Durkheim's formulation. Thomas Merton made a threefold distinction in his consideration of anomie:[44] culture goals, i.e., wants taught by the culture; norms that prescribe the means one may employ in the pursuit of goals; and actual distribution of facilities and opportunities for achieving the culture goals. The disjunction between the goals and means and the resulting strains lead to the weakening of men's commitments to culturally prescribed goals or institutionalized means. Thus, Merton's thesis that anomie is produced by strains inherent in the social structure presupposes a society that demands that all

---

43. *Ibid.* See also Albert Cohen, *Deviance and Control* (Englewood Cliffs, N. J.: Prentice Hall, 1966), pp. 74–75.
44. Thomas Merton, "Social Structure and Anomie," in *Social Theory and Social Structure* (Glencoe, Ill.: Free Press, 1957), pp. 128–94. See also Ephraim Misruchi, *Success and Opportunity* (Glencoe, Ill.: Free Press, 1964).

must compete.[45] The differential access to life's goals produces anomie. Meir and Bell substantiate this position, emphazing socially structured limitation in the access to means of achieving life's goals. The inability to achieve these goals follows mainly as a result of the individual's position in the social structure. The resultant discrepancies result in power differentials and differences in life's chances. Meir and Bell also conclude that anomie is not necessariy confined to city-dwellers or urban societies.[46]

Lewis Rhodes reached a different conclusion. Merton's thesis would lead one to predict that categories of persons with low status and high aspirations would have higher rates of anomie. Rhodes found that anomie occurs where the distance between aspirations and life's chances is maximized in both directions; i.e., anomie is high where status is low and hence when life-chances for success are high and aspirations are low. His conclusion is that the aspiration-status discrepancy is antecedent to anomie.[47]

Gwynn Nettler separates three related but nonidentical ideas, those of alienation, anomie, and personal disorganization. "An alienated person is one who has been estranged from and made unfriendly toward, his society and the culture it carries."[48] The focus then is on society.

McClosky and Scharr contend that anomie is governed not only by one's position and role in society but also by one's intellectual and personality characteristics. Consequently, persons whose cognitive capacity is deficient or those who are strongly governed by anxiety and hostility are more likely to view society as disorderly and bewilder-

---

45. *Ibid.*

46. Dorothy Meir and Wendell Bell, "Anomia and Differential Access to the Achievement of Life Goals," *ASR* (February 1959), pp. 189–202. See also Ephraim Misruchi, "Social Structure and Anomia in a Small City," *ASR* (August 1960), pp. 645–54.

47. Lewis Rhodes, "Anomia, Aspiration and Status," *Social Forces* (May 1964), pp. 434–40.

48. Gwynn Nettler, "A Measure of Alienation," *ASR* (December 1957), p. 670.

ing. Personality dispositions reduce the chances of inter-action and communication, hampering even more the learn-ing of societal norms. Hence, anomic feelings occur when socialization and the learning of the norms are impeded. Some impediments are social, but others are personal and psychological.[49] Morton Grodzins defines alienation as ". . . the state in which individuals feel no sense of belonging to their community or nation. Personal contacts are neither stable nor satisfactory."[50] He sees the alienated person as the "potentially disloyal citizen" and suggests that alienation will more probably occur in certain types of personalities and at certain levels of society.[51]

Another group of researchers looks to certain types of in-dividuals. C. C. Bowman associates scholarship with "some degree of isolation" and sees intellectuals as generally alien-ated from bourgeois culture.[52] Jan Hayda has tried to ac-count for the intellectual's alienation. There is, first, the attachment to abstract values. Second, the outside world is suspicious of him; therefore the intellectual sees that world as being destructive to him. Third, there is his self-emanci-pation from popular standards.[53]

Abscarian and Stanage feel that alienation is experienced in varying forms and degrees of intensity when certain forces block the individual's quest for authentic or true existence, when he "feels unable to shake off a sense of cleavage, of

49. Herbert McClosky and John Scharr "Psychological Dimension of Anomy," *ASR* (February 1965), pp. 14–40.
50. Morton Grodzins, *The Loyal and Disloyal* (Chicago, Ill.: University of Chicago Press, 1956), p. 134.
51. *Ibid.*
52. C. C. Bowman, "Is Sociology Too Detached?" *ASR* (October 1956), pp. 564–68.
53. Jan Hayda, "Alienation and the Integration of Student Intellectuals," *ASR* 28 (October 1966) : 759. See also T. M. Furst, "Anti Intellectualism and Lay Intelligentsia," (doctoral dissertation, University of California, 1958). Furst disagrees with the view that the professional thinker is different from others and does not bear the stigma of alienation. See also Nettler, p. 671, and A. W. Griswold, "Better Men and Better Mousetraps: The Scholar's Business in American Society," *Saturday Review* (November 1956), p. 10.

an abyss within himself, and between himself and others."[54]
Still another group of scholars seeks to explain alienation
in man's work. Erich Fromm makes alienation central to
the thesis of his *Sane Society* and, for him, the hallmark of
the alienated is his "marketing orienation," his regarding
the world and himself as commodities to which monetary
values may be assigned and which may be peddled.[55] Warner
and Abegglen relate such a marketing orientation of the big
business leader to the more customary conception of alienation as isolation from others. They say ". . . all of these
mobile men, as a necessary part of the equipment that
makes it possible for them to be mobile and leave people
behind without fear or regret, have difficulty in accepting
and imposing the kinds of reciprocal obligations that close
friendship and intimate social contacts imply. They typically
are isolated men."[56] Joel Nelson found owners are more
likely to be anomic than managers because of their "differential commitments to social and geographical mobility."[57]

Robert Blauner maintains that work permitting autonomy, responsibility, and social connection furthers the dignity of individuals, whereas work devoid of such features
restricts their development and therefore is negatively
valued. He attempts to reduce the idea of alienation to
clear-cut empirical concepts. He sees industrial powerlessness as incorporating four elements: first, the inability to
influence general managerial policies; second, the lack of
control over the conditions of employment; third, the lack
of control of the immediate work process; fourth, alienation
as related to the ownership of the means of production. For
America only numbers two and three would have rele-

54. Gilbert Abscarian and S. Stanage, "Alienation and the Radical Right,"
Journal of Politics (November 1965), pp. 766-96.
55. Erich Fromm, *The Sane Society* (New York: Holt & Rinehart, 1955).
56. W. L. Warner and J. C. Abegglen, *Big Business Leaders in America*
(New York: Harper and Row, 1955), p. 90.
57. Joel Nelson, "Comparisons Between the Old and New Middle Class,"
AJS (September 1968), pp. 184-92.

vance.[58] According to Marx, however, the very restrictions of a worker's interests to immediate activity only is the product of capitalism, which transforms the human being into the simple agent of production. To Marx the worker's psychology was but a derivative of the mode and relations of production.[59] Aiken and Hage found that highly centralized and highly formalized organizational structures are characterized by greater work alienation and greater alienation from expressive relations.[60]

How alienation is manifested politically has been dealt with in a number of studies, with mixed results. Morris Rosenberg asserts that feelings of being alone and weak, and feelings of fatalism, would tend to make a person apathetic politically.[61] Herbert Goldhamer has speculated that persons who have a relatively high level of personal anxiety and who use all of their psychic energy for that concern are unlikely to divert energy to political activity.[62] Dwight Dean found a positive correlation between powerlessness, normlessness, social isolation, and total alienation. His findings do not support the view of Rosenberg that a sense of powerlessness is related to political apathy nor do they support Lazarsfeld and Lubell's, that normlessness is related to apathy, nor Lazarsfeld's contention that social isolation is highly related to nonvoting.[63] Robert Agger concluded that persons who feel cynical about politics are much less likely to be participators. This attitude may attempt to justify itself in the following: loss of faith in the qualifications of

58. Robert Blauner, *Alienation and Freedom* (Chicago: University of Chicago Press, 1964).
59. Igor Kon, "The Concept of Alienation in Modern Sociology," *Social Research* (Autumn 1967), pp. 507–28.
60. M. Aiken and J. Hage, "Organizational Alienation: A Comparative Analysis," *ASR* 31 (August 1966): pp. 497–507.
61. Morris Rosenberg, "The Meaning of Politics in Mass Society," *POQ* (Spring 1951). See also "Some Determinants of Political Apathy," *POQ* (Winter 1954).
62. Herbert Goldhamer, "Public Opinion and Personality," *AJS* (January 1950).
63. Dwight Dean, "Alienation and Political Apathy," *Social Forces* (March 1960), pp. 185–89.

voters; the lack of responsiveness on the part of legislators to the opinions of voters; the lack of integrity of candidates; the fear of unrestricted freedom of speech; the use of the state as an instrument of restriction. He found no difference in the degree of political cynicism among Republicans, Democrats, and Independents. He found no relation with social class, although educational attainment was more strongly related to political cynicism than was income.[64] A sense of political impotency goes hand-in-hand with a cynical view of politics.[65] Edgar Litt found formal education strongly related to political efficacy and an equally strong relationship with political trust. The institutionalization of political cynicism to Litt may "bolster a modicum of self efficacy to the extent it supports the fragmentation of power networks . . . and the insularity of ethnic politics."[66]

Still another series of studies suggests that persons living in communities with urban political machines are more likely to develop cynical attitudes toward politics than those who live in communities without urban machines. Murray Levin distinguishes alienation from anomie by noting that the former refers to a psychological state of an individual characterized by feelings of estrangement. The alienated is "acutely aware of the discrepancy between who he is and what he believes he should be."[67] Levin notes that there are four aspects of alienation: powerlessness, meaninglessness, estrangement, and the lowering of norms. He sees the causes of alienation in the "disjunction of political values and structures."[68] He asserts that the classical theory of democracy does not fit the conditions of the real world,

---

64. Robert Agger *et al.*, "Political Cynicism: Measurement Meaning," *Journal of Politics* (August 1951) . See also M. Rosenberg, "Misanthropy and Political Ideology," *ASR* (December 1956) .

65. Edgar Litt, "Political Cynicism and Political Futility," *Journal of Politics* 25 (May 1963) : 312-323.

66. *Ibid.*

67. Murray Levin, *The Alienated Voter* (New York: Holt, Rinehart and Winston, 1960) , p. 59.

68. *Ibid.*

leading to exaggerated expectations. Schattschneider observes that the alienated may see the role of institutions as discriminatory rather than discriminating. The institutional nature of the operating political system may serve to reinforce the alienated feelings of the individual.[69]

Other researchers use powerlessness measures. Thompson and Horton operationally define political alienation as a feeling of powerlessness and an identification of an appropriate power center as a controlling agent. They observe, ". . . political inefficacy may result in political alienation and, not only apathy or indifference as a response to awareness of powerlessness, but also diffuse displeasure at being powerless and being mistrustful of those who wield power. Political alienation may be expected to be translated into either an undirected vote of resentment or an organized vote of resentment or an organized vote of opposition."[70] They not only find the expected relationship between the composite index of powerlessness and negative voting, but they present some evidence that the feeling of powerlessness by itself has an independent effect on voting behavior.[71] Aberbach concludes, "Clearly, on these local issues, a perceived sense of powerlessness does lead to negative voting or to opposition to certain controversial programs. However, it is not certain just what effect distrust of local government exerts and how it interacts with feelings of powerlessness." Aberbach also notes that while research on and knowledge of the relationship between alienation and vote are incomplete on local elections, there is even less known about that relationship in national elections.[72] Templeton

---

69. E. E. Schattschneider, *The Semi Sovereign People* (New York: Holt, Rinehart and Winston, 1960) .

70. Wayne Thompson and John Horton, "Political Alienation as a Force in Political Action," *Social Forces* (March 1960) , pp. 190–95. See also Eckhardt and Hendershot, "Transformation of Alienation into Public Opinion," *Sociological Quarterly* (Autumn 1968) , pp. 459–67. M. Olsen, "Alienation and Public Opinion," *POQ* (Summer 1965) , pp. 200–212.

71. Nettler, 670–77.

72. Aberbach, p. 90.

found some inferential support for the notion that the "quality" of the vote cast by an alienated voter may be different; i.e., that he tends to cast a negative vote and is most inspired when issues are perceived in terms of good and evil. According to Templeton, the process as practiced in this country serves to insulate us from direct impact of the alienated feelings of part of the electorate.[73]

Melvin Seeman found a direct relationship between powerlessness, alienation, and organizational membership.[74] This author in his study of an American university concluded that most students would assume passive spectator roles rather than organizing or initiating political action. While there was significant dissatisfaction with the University's goals, there was only a mild support for them. The author found,

A high sense of powerlessness in the decision-making process was evident in all groups . . . The apathetic tend to withdraw, but are brought out on certain issues . . . The activists will take part in more militant political action. Dissatisfaction, low organizational membership, low interest in changing policies makes it possible for this latter group to exert an influence out of proportion to its numbers. It is possible that this group will be able to convert a passive student body to support its goal on a university issue . . .[75]

Some studies have found a correlation between cynicism and education.[76] McDill and Ridley found education, anomie and political alienation significantly related to voting behavior on a metropolitan issue.[77]

73. Frederic Templeton, "Alienation and Political Participation," *POQ* (Summer 1966) , pp. 252–55.
74. Melvin Seeman, "Alienation, Membership and Political Knowledge: A Comparative Study," *POQ* (Fall 1966) , pp. 353–67.
75. Patrick J. Gallo, "Student Alienation at an American University," *Rassegna Italiana di Sociologia* (April 1970) , p. 309.
76. Arthur Kornhauser, *When Labor Votes* (New York: University Books, 1956) . See also Agger, "Political Cynicism; Measurement and Meaning"; Angus Campbell, "The Passive Citizen," *Acta Sociologica* (1962) . Campbell disputes this finding.
77. Edward McDill and Jeanne Ridley, "Status, Anomia, Political Alienation and Political Participation," *AJS* (1968) , pp. 205–13.

Aberbach reports that factor analysis confirmed the dimensionality of several different measures of alienation. His data support the usefulness of considering specific types of political alienation separately.[78] Ada Finfiter found that there were significant differences in the variables that are associated with each type of alienation.

Individuals with high powerlessness scores are unlikely to participate in community activities. . . . They are likely to be older, to have less education, and to have low faith in people. Conversely, living in smaller communities or being Jewish are characteristics that tend to reduce this type of alienation. High scores on the perceived normlessness scale are most likely for individuals with low faith in people, who are native born, . . . live in large cities, or attend church infrequently.[79]

Finfiter concluded that there may be conditions that impel those normally not alienated in either way to a state of "extreme disengagement."

78. Aberbach, pp. 93–98.
79. Ada Finfiter, "Dimensions of Political Alienation," *APSR* (June 1970), p. 405.

Ethnic Alienation
The Italian-Americans

1

Neighborhood and Community

In the following discussion the main concern is in the formation and persistence of an ethnic subsociety. The ethnic enclave is viewed as a particular response to a set of stimuli interacting with a number of predispositions. The persistence of the ethnic enclave is evidence of the feedback that occurs from response to stimulus to predisposition.

The decided urban preference on the part of an ethnic group is in part owing to earlier patterns of immigration and residence. In particular, the size of the metropolitan area, the distance from the central city, and the numerical size of the ethnic group are major determinants of an urban concentration.

The urban concentration of an ethnic group encourages the establishment and survival of an ethnic enclave. In addition, quota laws that required proof of sponsorship perpetuated the ethnic enclave.[1] A family-link type of immigration

---

1. The rationale behind the quota laws is one example of an outgroup rejection. It was also one vehicle by which the host society conveyed its role expectations to the newcomers. Ironically, it perpetuated the very thing to which the host society so strongly objected, namely, the ethnic enclave.

is a vital factor in both the urban preference of an ethnic group and the group's residential stability.

An ethnic group coming from a rural to an urban setting is less able to cope with the new environment than one moving from an urban to an urban setting. A major determinant in the formation of the ethnic enclave is an outgroup rejection. The enclave fulfills the psychological need for security and satisfaction, so that the rejected urban ethnic may move with confidence toward interaction with the larger society.

Residential patterns are altered only as a result of movement into the higher socioeconomic categories, outgroup acceptance and assimilation.[2]

Residential Patterns among Italian-Americans

In the discussion that follows, an attempt will be made

		TABLE I	
Year	Immigrants	Naturalized Immigrants	Resident Aliens
1957	19,061	9,056	
1958	24,479	8,462	
1959	16,251	8,079	
1960	14,933	14,560	257,477
1961	20,652	18,362	248,733
1962	21,442	17,449	234,229
1963	16,588	12,171	228,766
1964	13,245	12,323	225,320
1965	10,821	10,742	214,618
1966	25,154	10,981	210,649
1967	26,565	10,481	223,357
1968	23,593	9,379	226,830
1969	23,617	8,773	241,230
1970	24,973	7,892	247,380
1971	22,137	7,576	244,932

Source: U. S. Annual Report, 1957–71, Immigration & Naturalization Service.

---

2. I shall discuss later the impact of a structural separation on the ethnic subsociety.

to paint in broad brush strokes a portrait of the residence and immigration patterns of the Italian immigrant.

An average of 23,000 Italian immigrants have come to the United States annually in the years since 1967 (Table I). During the period from 1958 to 1969, a total of 89,244 Italian immigrants settled in the United States. The total Italian stock, which includes the first and second generation, was 4,543,935, or 2.53% of the total population. The Italians Italians who were born in Italy comprise 0.7% of the American population, but 13.7% of the foreign-born population.[3]

Sixty-nine percent of the total population of the United States reside in urban areas as compared to 91.8% of all the Italians. This underscores the urban concentration of the Italian stock (Table II).

The regional distribution of Italians is also instructive. The northeast region contains 70.3% of the Italian-born and 69.2 of the native-born of Italian parentage (Table III). Thus, a total of 69.5% of the Italian stock reside in this region.[4] The persistence of this pattern is made clearer when we consider that Robert Foerester, in his monumental study of the mass immigration period, found that 71.8% of all Italians resided in the' New England and Middle Atlantic areas.[5]

The area from north of Boston to south of Norfolk, the

---

3. U. S. Immigration and Naturalization Service, *Annual Report* (Washington, 1966, 1967, 1968, 1969). According to the U. S. Census definition, those residents of the U. S. born in Italy are considered first generation. The native born of Italian parentage are second generation. The classification of Italian stock thus includes first and second generation. The third generation is not counted.

4. U. S. Census of Population, 1960. Summary Volume.

5. Robert Foerester, *The Italian Immigration of Our Times* (Cambridge: Harvard University Press, 1919), p. 329. For an overall summary of Italian immigration see *National Bureau of Economic Research*, "International Migration," (Washington, 1929), vols. 1 and 2; Giovanni Schiavo, *The Italians in Chicago* (Chicago: Italian American Publishing Co., 1928), p. 141. For a regional distribution by the section of origin during the mass immigration, see Report of the Immigration Commission, *Statistical Review of Immigration* (Washington: GPO, 1911), pp. 14–44, "Italian Emigration Over A Century: Various Aspects and Characteristics," *Emigration Report #35* (Rome) (March–April 1962), p. 3828.

TABLE II

	Total	Urban	Rural Non-Farm	Rural Farm
Total Population	179,323,175	69.7	22.6	7.5
Foreign Stock	34,050,406	83.7	12.6	3.7
Italian Stock	4,543,935	91.8	7.4	.8
Foreign Born of Italian Mother Tongue	1,226,141	93.4	5.7	.9

Source: U. S. Bureau of Census, 1960. General Characteristics of Population.

so-called megalopolis, contains about 20% of the total population and 70% of all Italians. Sixteen states have 94% of the Italian stock and 95% of the Italian born (Table IV). These same states contained 96.4% of the Italian aliens in 1965. Of the Italian immigrants who arrived between 1960 to 1965, 65% preferred the Northeast region. A total of 72.6% of all the resident Italian aliens in early 1965 were registered in the Northeast.

That 82.2% of all Italians reside in Standard Metropolitan areas and 31.6% in the smaller cities underscores the urban preference of the Italian immigrant (Table V).

The size of the metropolitan area and its distance from New York are determinants of the degree of urban concentration for Italian immigrants. Twenty-three Standard Metropolitan Statistical areas had more than 25,000 people of Italian stock each, which includes the cities of the megalopolis (Table V). According to Dr. Velikonja, "The numerical size alone permits the establishment of many Italian cultural and social services and contributes also to the longer survival of the Italian cultural character in cases where the relative position of the Italian group is not very strong."[6]

When we compare the total Italian stock with that of the total population in the major cities, the dominance of New York and Connecticut becomes immediately apparent, since Italians form more than 10% of the entire population. New

6. Dr. Joseph Velikonja, "Italian Immigrants in the U. S. in the Mid Sixties," *International Migration Review* (Summer 1967), p. 33. (Hereinafter cited as *IMR*.)

TABLE III. REGIONAL DISTRIBUTION OF THE ITALIAN

	Italian born 1st gen T	%	Native born of Italian parentage	2nd-gen %	Italian Stock 1st & 2nd gen T	%	Italian T	Aliens %
Northeast	883,074	70.3	2,273,235	69.2	3,156,309	69.5	156,201	72.6
North Central	190,686	15.2	486,982	14.8	677,668	14.5	30,349	14.3
South	58,239	4.6	208,059	6.2	266,298	5.9	9,273	4.4
West	125,000	9.9	318,660	9.2	443,660	9.8	18,765	8.7
Total	1,256,900	100	3,286,936	100	4,543,935	100	214,618	100
% of total population		0.7		1.8		2.5		0.1

Source: U. S. Census of Population, 1960. Summary Volume.
U. S. Immigration & Naturalization. Aliens in the U. S., 1965.

Haven is the highest-ranked metropolitan area,[7] where the Italians constituted 15.8% of the total population (Table V). The New York-New Jersey consolidated area has a total of 10.3%, while in many of the cities the number is higher. Jersey City had 13.6%. Richmond, Kings, and Paterson-Clifton-Passaic each had 14.1%. Of the foreign-born population, one eighth were Italian in Fair Lawn, one third in Paterson, and one tenth in Ridgewood, New Jersey. Special mention is made of these communities, since members of the control group were drawn from them.[8] More than a quarter of Bergen county's foreign-stock residents are of Italian origin. This constitutes the largest bloc of ethnic Italians in the state of New Jersey. Nearly one-quarter of the foreign stock is Italian in the eight-county area of New Jersey closest to New York City, which includes the following counties: Bergen, Hudson, Passaic, Essex, Morris, Union, Middlesex, and Somerset. In New York City 20.7% of the total foreign-born population and 8.6% of the foreign stock is Italian.[9] Approximately 6% of the foreign-born population in the Bronx is Italian, 5% in Brooklyn, 10% in Manhattan, 5% in Queens, and 3% in Richmond.[10] The heavy concentration in the New York area was also noted in the mass immigration era by Foerester.

In the state of New York were about as many Italians as the whole country had contained ten years earlier. Two out of five of all the newcomers, in recent years, have gone thither. Of those in the state in 1910, nearly two thirds dwelt in its metropolis, 340,770—such a number as would make one of the large cities in Italy; and if their children were added, the

---

7. U. S. Census of Population, 1960, Part 34, Vol. I (Table 79), See Tables VII and VIII. Also see U. S. Census of Population, 1970.

8. *Ibid.*, pp. 275–81, Part 32.

9. These figures represent those born in Italy or born in the United States of a parent who was born in Italy. Thus, it only includes first- and second-generation Americans of Italian origin and not third or fourth generations. Consequently the number of Italian-Americans in these cases may even be larger.

10. Ninth Annual Statistical Guide for New York City, Department of Commerce and Industrial Development of N. Y. C. (1965), pp. 33–35.

TABLE IV. ITALIANS IN NINE PRINCIPAL STATES

State	Italian Stock 1960	Italian Born 1960	Italian Aliens 1965
New York	1,476,946	440,063	84,081
New Jersey	525,100	137,356	23,490
Pennsylvania	509,314	131,149	17,193
California	348,414	102,366	15,679
Connecticut	237,146	65,233	14,825
Illinois	249,873	72,139	13,765
Massachusetts	311,053	86,921	13,262
Michigan	120,363	36,879	6,608
Ohio	185,492	50,338	5,978

Source: U. S. Census of Population, 1960.

TABLE V. ITALIANS IN MAJOR METROPOLITAN AREAS, 1960

	Italian Stock	First Generation	Second Generation	Italian Stock as % of total population
New York-N. J.	1,531,352	453,929	1,077,423	10.3
Philadelphia, Pa.	248,558	63,570	184,988	5.7
Boston, Mass.	202,987	57,718	145,269	7.8
Pittsburgh, Pa.	138,429	36,754	101,675	5.7
Buffalo, N. Y.	77,434	20,441	56,993	5.9
Providence, R. I.	76,580	18,200	58,380	9.4
Rochester, N. Y.	57,134	17,047	40,089	9.7
New Haven, Conn.	49,172	11,727	37,395	15.8
Albany-Schenectady-Troy	41,611	11,471	30,140	6.3
Hartford, Conn.	39,812	12,303	27,509	7.6
Syracuse, N. Y.	35,165	9,398	25,767	6.2
Utica-Rome, N.Y.	30,192	7,659	22,533	9.1
Waterbury, Conn.	25,987			14.3

Source: U. S. Census of Population, 1960.

colony would exceed in population every Italian city, except possibly Naples. . . . About four fifths of all the Italians were classed by the census as urban, twice as high a proportion as for the country's population as a whole.[11]

11. Foerester, p. 329. See Table VI.

Today the Italians continue to live in the central city in significant numbers. As in Foerester's early description, the urban concentration of Italians today does not coincide with the general trend of the American cities, which has seen an increased flight from the central city and a reduced growth of the entire eastern seaboard. According to Dr. Velikonja, the reason for the high urban concentration is "the legislative provision for the quota and non quota immigrants which require the sponsorship or the documentation of parentage for admission to the United States. The legislative restrictions, therefore, aiming to prevent the establishment of national clusters through national quota restrictions, instead reinforced these same concentrations by requiring sponsorship or proof of parentage. Therefore, the general regional pattern which was established in its essence at the turn of the century is being unduly perpetuated for much longer than is economically and culturally advisable."[12] In addition, the early residence patterns of the mass immigrants, along with the family-link immigration patterns of the present, further reinforce the urban preferences of Italian immigrants. Italian immigration is part of an overall rural-to-urban flow that is affecting Italy profoundly. It is likely that had the immigrants not chosen to come to an urban area in America they would have done so in Italy.[13] Italian immigration, then, is another dimension of the Italian rural-urban flow.

Formation of the Italian-American Subsociety

Based upon the extensive distribution of a number of peasant traits, such as Banfield's "amoral familism,"[14] some

---

12. Velikonja, p. 32.
13. "Research and Notes," *IMR* 1 (Fall 1966) : 48–49. See also Robert Fried, "Urbanization and Italian Politics," *Journal of Politics* 29 (August 1967) : 505–34.
14. Edward C. Banfield, *The Moral Basis of a Backward Society* (Glencoe, Ill.: The Free Press, 1958) .

assert that Italy is still a peasant society. According to Fried,

Italy under this theory would be nothing but "Montegrano" writ large. . . . This can hardly be the case if, as is reported by Italian rural sociologists, Montegrano itself has become highly atypical of Italian rural towns.[15]

TABLE VI. ITALIAN IMMIGRATION TO MAJOR CITIES

NEW YORK—NEW JERSEY

	1966	1967	1968
Elizabeth	133	134	124
Jersey City	289	174	224
Newark	378	397	259
Paterson	90	295	415
Trenton	4	80	80
Albany	99	105	99
Buffalo	198	197	165
N.Y.C.	7,382	7,971	6,764
Rochester	436	567	340
Syracuse	110	132	111
Yonkers	165	163	153

Source: U. S. Immigration and Naturalization Annual Report, 1966, 1967, 1968.

TABLE VII. STATES OF INTENDED RESIDENCE

	1966	1967	1968	1969
New York	10,635	11,661	9,747	
New Jersey	3,315	3,252	3,150	

Source: U. S. Iimmigration and Naturalization, Annual Report, 1966, 1967, 1968.

TABLE VIII. DECLARED DESTINATION OF IMMIGRANTS

1960–65

	Total	Percent of Total
New York	30,951	28.9
Chicago	6,452	6.0
Newark-Paterson	3,699	3.4
Philadelphia	3,075	2.9

---

15. Fried, p. 512.

Rochester	2,053	1.9
Boston-Cambridge	1,896	1.8
Detroit	1,532	1.4
Cleveland	1,255	1.2
Pittsburgh	1,052	1.0
San Francisco-Oakland	986	.9
Hartford	939	.9
Los Angeles	936	.9
	54,826	51.2

Source: U. S. Immigration and Naturalization, Annual Report, 1960, 1961, 1962, 1964, 1965, Table 12B.

Particularly in northern areas one may still find Italian peasants living in isolated towns. All of my immigrant respondents had attended the cinema at least once in their lifetime. For most it was a frequent occurrence. Polizzi found that half of his rural respondents had never attended the cinema.[16] Of my immigrant respondents, fourteen viewed television regularly. Fifty-three percent of his respondents held that they had viewed T.V. either on a daily basis or at least two or three times a week. Thirteen of my immigrant respondents had visited a large city at least ten times a year. Italians, particularly in the South, tend to live in compact and sizable communities, as did my respondents. Many of the Italian industrial workers live in rural areas surrounding the few major industrial centers. The result "is an unusual disparity between the degree of Italian urbanization and the degree of industrialization."[17] According to Stuart Hughes, ". . . in a country so urban in its traditions as Italy—and at the same time so heavily rural—the misunderstanding and latent hostitlity between city and country have been peculiarly intense."[18] Southern towns, even those with as many as 35,000 or even 50,000, are inhabited to some

---

16. Anthony Polizzi, "Southern Italy: Its Peasantry and Change" (Ph.D. dissertation, Cornell University, 1968), pp. 211–12. See Question 3a, interview schedule.

17. Fried, p. 511.

18. Stuart Hughes, The United States and Italy (Cambridge, Mass.: Harvard University Press, 1965), p. 40.

extent by peasant families, while urbanization in the North has been accompanied by the development of modern industry, commerce, and agriculture. Southern provincial capitals have grown 29 times as much as those of lesser cities.[19] Seventy-five percent of their growth, however, comes from natural causes rather than a rural exodus.

The rural to urban flow is most significant to the north and other industrial centers of Europe, Canada, and the United States.[20] An estimated four million southerners went North between 1945 and 1964.[21] Migration has been a familiar form of escape for the Italian population. Today's migration represents a major move in the peasant's life. The city represents freedom from the restriction of the rural village for greater self-expression.[22]

By some criteria the South is urbanized, if one means by that term centers of 2,000 to 5,000 people. If, on the other hand, one defines *urban* as centers of the population not engaged in agriculture, the South then is less urbanized. It is not heavily urbanized if one means a community with certain public facilities, a sizable number of the labor force in modern industry, and commerce, with a distinctive way of life and producing a distinctive type of social character. By the first and second definitions, the Italian immigrants interviewed came with something of an urban outlook. All of the immigrant respondents seemed to indicate that their horizons were not limited to the village. Visits to large cities occurred often. If they had remained in Italy, they indicated that they would have moved to a large city somewhere in the North. Thus, the movement from a less urban south

---

19. Manilio Rossi Doria, "Aspetti sociali dello sviluppo economico in Italia," *Atti del IV Congresso Mondiale di Sociologia* (Bari) (1959), pp. 9–35.

20. Research & Notes, IMR, pp. 48–49.

21. Domenico De Masi, "Migrazioni e congiuntura a Milano," *Nord e Sud* (October 1964), pp. 62–86.

22. Polizzi, p. 105. See also Sydel Silverman, "Agricultural Organization, Social Structure, and Values in Italy: Amoral Familism Reconsidered," *American Anthropologist* (February 1964), pp. 16–17. The city also presents problems of finding employment, identity, etc. A different form of systematic organization is also needed.

to urban America is part of the rural-to-urban flow.

Eight of the new arrivals interviewed were born in towns of 5,000 or less (Table IX). Of that number, seven lived in the same town in which they were born prior to coming to the United States, while only one took up residence in a city of over 100,000 before his departure. Six of the new arrivals were born in towns with populations between 20,000 to 50,000 and resided there before departure. Only one respondent was born and resided before departure in a city of 50,000 to 100,000 people.[23]

Even during the mass immigration, Veccoli tells us, "The typical south Italian peasant . . . did not live in a small village, but in a 'rural city' with a population of thousands or even tens of thousands. Seeking refuge from brigands and malaria, the contadini huddled together in these hill towns, living in stone dwellings under the most primitive conditions and each day descending the slopes to work in the fields."[24] But during the mass immigration the "rural city" formed the social center and circumscribed the social horizon of most southern Italians. It depended in most cases upon its own resources for economic support and was almost a complete entity in itself. The topography contributed to this isolation.

The term campanilismo, meaning that which is within the sound of the village bell, was an appropriate name given by the natives to this regionalism. Redfield notes that

the prestige of the town, the polis, carried with it at an early date the peasant's distaste for agricultural life. The South Italian may bring a distaste for rural life down from ancient times, while he also is influenced by the fact that he now lives in hardship in contrast to the life of the gentry and the rich.[25]

---

23. Questions 1, 2, 3, interview schedule.
24. Rudolph J. Veccoli, "Contadini in Chicago: A Critique of the Uprooted," *Journal of American History* (December 1964), p. 405.
25. Robert Redfield, *Peasant Society and Culture* (Chicago: University of Chicago Press, 1956), pp. 66–67.

TABLE IX. SIZE OF COMMUNITY OF BIRTH AND CURRENT RESIDENCE

	5,000 or less		5,000–10,000		20,000–50,000		50,000–100,000		100,000 or over	
	Birth	Current Residence	Birth	Current Residence	Birth	Current Residence	Birth	Current Residence	Birth	Current Residence
Immigrants	8				6		1			15
Italian-Americans First Gen.					4				1	5
Italian-Americans Second Gen.									5	5
Italian-Americans Third Gen.									5	5

The city has had a great impact upon Italian Society. Another observer has stated,

> There is no other nation whose tradition, legends and popular epic are compelled so constantly to look to the city for their origin. . . . This voluntary binding of the peasant to the city, that exists almost everywhere in Italy, is one of the permanent strands of the Italian social fabric.[26]

Southern Italy today is no longer the peasant society of the mass emigration. The economic development of the South by the "Cassa per il messogiorno"[27] and the penetration of modern communications and transportation into the countryside have changed the character of rural life. They have had an impact on the values, institutions, and expectations of southern Italians in particular.

The movement from rural areas to the cities assumed torrential proportions during the late 1950s. Forty-two percent of the labor force in 1951 was found to be engaged in agriculture, while in 1961 it decreased to 32% and in 1963 to 25%.[28] Over a million people left for the cities between 1950 and 1960.[29] Of the Italian population in Italy in 1951, 32.2% held residence in towns different from the ones in which they had been born.[30]

Aside from the economic motives, southern Italians are moving to the city to evade the strong group ties and clearcut social class distinctions that characterized their former residence.[31] People living in the countryside are losing their rural culture. They find themselves uprooted as a whole new set of values submerges the rural way of life and a new way

26. Carlo Sforza, *Italy and the Italians* (New York: E. P. Dutton and Co., Inc., 1949) .
27. Fund for the development of the South.
28. *L'Espresso*, October 15, 1961, pp. 17–19; April 8, 1962, p. 5.
29. *L'Espresso*, July 30, 1961, p. 2.
30. Aldo Predetti. *Le Componenti economiche, sociali e demografiche della mobilita interna della populazione italiana* (Milan: Vita e Pensiero, 1965) , pp. 60–65.
31. *Ibid.*

of life emerges. The movement from the rural areas to the urban centers should make the individual better able to empathize with other Italians and groups in Italian society.[32] His literacy should increase and he should engage in more meaningful participation in the political process. Urbanization will tend to make the Italian less parochial and traditional.

Of the fifteen Italian immigrants interviewed, there were twelve men and three women, of an average age of 29. Since 1966 there has been a relatively even distribution of the sexes among Italian immigrants.[33] The great bulk of the immigrants who have come in the last four years were between ten and forty years old.[34] Of the first-generation respondents, there were four men and one woman, of average age of twenty-seven. Both groups of second- and third-generation Italian-Americans consisted of three men and two women; in the former case the average age was forty-one, in the latter, twenty-six.

Four of the first-generation respondents were born in cities of 20,000 to 50,000, only one having been born in a city larger than 100,000[35] (Table IX). All were residing in cities of 100,000 or more at the time they were interviewed. All of the Italian-American respondents indicated that any future movement would be within the same city. Most of the second- and third-generation respondents lived in the same town in which they were born. The greatest disparity in size of community of birth and size of community of current residence occurs in the group of newly arrived and that of the first generation. Most immigrant and first-generation respondents go to large cities, particularly large industrial and commercial centers. As we scan the second- and third-generation residence, we see a greater urban concentration.

32. Daniel Lerner, *The Passing of Traditional Society* (Glencoe, Ill.: The Free Press, 1958).
33. *Ibid.*
34. *Emigration Report #35*, p. 3827.
35. Questions 2 and 3, interview schedule.

The greatest movement is in the first generation, with a relative stability emerging into the second and third generation.

This relative residential stability is seen in the first Italian neighborhoods, which have clung to their identity. East Harlem, Greenwich Village, Mulberry and Mott Streets, Carrol Gardens, Bay Ridge, and Red Hook are all "Italian neighborhoods." Nathan Kantrowitz found that though ethnic segregation has weakened in New York City, "the reports of its demise are exaggerated."[36] Moreover, he found a correlation between Chicago and New York when each of the twelve ethnicities and races were ranked in their segregation from the base population. In his view, neither Chicago nor any other city differs substantially from New York in the pattern of ethnic segregation. Kantrowitz observed, "Two ethnicities remain highly segregated from all others: the Italians and Scandinavians. We might expect that the Italians, a southern European or new stock, would remain highly segregated but we would have no reason to anticipate that they are more integrated with the 'old' northwestern Europeans than with the 'new' southern and central Europeans."[37]

Fourteen of the Italian immigrants interviewed came to the United States through a link with a member of either the nuclear or extended family. This fact illustrates the importance of the family in southern Italian society. Moreover, it helps to explain not only the formation of the Italian neighborhood, but its persistence. Alfredo recalled, "My father's brother called him from Italy. My father came first. He then called the rest of us here. We stayed with my uncle in Jersey City and then my father's work brought us all to Brooklyn. After I got married we stayed in the neighborhood."[38] Alfredo's description of his arrival is typical not

36. Nathan Kantrowitz, "Ethnic Segregation in New York City," *AJS* (May 1969) , pp. 685–95.
37. *Ibid.*
38. Interview, Alfredo (machinist) . Question 6, interview schedule.

only of the Italian immigrants interviewed but of many who
are coming to America at present. It is also typical of how
Alfredo's uncle came to America. It is reminiscent of the
family chain of immigration that operated during the days
of the mass immigration. The male usually arrived first
through a relative or a *paesano*, established himself with
others from his town or province, and then proceeded to
call for the rest of his family.[39]

All of the immigrant respondents lived with other new
arrivals in exclusively Italian neighborhoods. William F.
Whyte has noted this development: "The paesani tend to
settle in one area, and those who are members of the same
family usually live close together."[40] Herbert Gans referred
to this area as the urban village. An area of first or second
settlement for urban migrants who try to "adapt their non-
urban institutions and culture to the urban milieu" is, often
described "in ethnic terms: Little Italy, The Ghetto, or
Black Belt."[41] Gans then notes their subsequent movements
as follows: ". . . almost all of the West Enders came to the
area as part of a group. Even their movements within the
West End . . . had been made together with other Italians
at about the same time.[42] The length of residence of the immigrant respondents ranged from two and one half weeks
to six years, which was also comparable to the time they
lived in the neighborhood. Only two of them said they preferred to live in a mixed neighborhood. Their concept of

39. Lawrence Pisani, *The Italian in America* (New York: Exposition Press,
1957). See also John Dickinson, "Aspects of Italian Immigration to Philadelphia," *Pennsylvania Magazine of History and Biography* (October 1966), p.
458; John MacDonald and Lentrice MacDonald, "Urbanization, Ethnic
Groups, and Social Segmentation," *Social Research* (Winter 1962), p. 434;
and Phyllis Williams, *South Italian Folkways in Europe and America* (New
Haven: Yale University Press, 1938), p. 17.

40. William F. Whyte, *Street Corner Society* (Chicago: University of Chicago Press, 1943), p. 208.

41. Herbert Gans, *The Urban Villagers* (New York: The Free Press, 1962),
p. 4. Gans fails to take into account the many changes in the Italian immigration. Italy, especially since the end of World War II, has experienced an
intensive rural-to-urban movement. Perhaps a more apt title of Gan's would
be *The Village Urbanists*.

42. *Ibid.*, p. 19.

a mixed neighborhood, from the examples given, was either Italian-American or areas occuped by immigrants from different regions of Italy.

When the immigrants of the mass immigration settled in New York or in the many industrial communities around the city, they tended to congregate with others from the same province or village.[43] This became the basis of the Italian neighborhood, which existed almost as a small semi-independent universe of its own. Sometimes physical lines separated the Italians from the rest of the population. There were also the invisible lines of separation. The family chain of immigration tended to reinforce the formation of the ethnic enclave. In addition was the Italian attachment to the town, in a word—companilismo.[44] The importance of coming to live with relatives and paesani from the same town took on new meaning in a strange environment. The immigrant was accustomed to identifying himself with others of the same village while in Italy and now found an increased desire for the same surroundings. In the crowded cities one could see the transfer of an entire village within a three- or four-block area. In some cases there was a block-by-block separation of Neapolitans, Calabrians, and Sicilians. As Pisani observes,

It was as if part of the old communities had been bodily transplanted to an American street. Signs and posters were in the Italian language, Italian tradesmen set up shop and peddlers sold Italian food through the streets.[45]

Foerester also takes note of this regionalism:

In Briey, in New York, in Buenos Aires, something like a street by street separation of the immigrants according to origin

---

43. Pisani, p. 125.
44. Phyllis Williams, p. 17.
45. Pisani, p. 61.

has been . . . recognizable . . . a thing so characteristically Italian that it is best denoted by . . . campanilismo.[46]

The original enclave started in or near the city's core was characterized by the movement of economically successful newcomers out of the enclave and into the "American" community. "Isolated from the community at large by differences in background and language, by their late arrival, and by their early low economic positions, they had to remain with themselves."[47] The lack of acceptance by the American society, the intense discrimination, the near-hysterical outburst of fear of the "Italian problem," and the militant nativism all served to reinforce the ethnic enclave.[48]

Some of the dwellings in which the immigrant respondents were housed were inhabited by earlier Italian immigrants. A number of the immigrant respondents lived in a six- or seven-block area of South Brooklyn with others who came from the same town.[49] The enclave is replete with local merchants, local club, and church, the latter with its bell tower standing symbolically if not protectively in the heart of the enclave. While this is some great modification of the ethnic enclaves of the earlier immigration, it is still identifiable as Italian.

The existence of a strong community among immigrants and its importance in the process of assimilation have be-

---

46. Foerester, p. 431. See also Humbert Nelli, "Italians in Urban America: A Study in Ethnic Adjustment," *IMR* (Summer 1967), pp. 38–55. Professor Nelli contends that it is an error to conclude that certain districts were either inhabited exclusively or even predominantly by Italians. Urban areas according to this view had few solidly Italian blocks or Italian neighborhoods.

47. Pisani, p. 125.

48. Salvatore Mondello, "The Italian Immigrant in Urban America 1880–1920, As Reported in the Contemporary Periodical Press" (doctoral dissertation, New York University, 1960). Professor Mondello concludes that a considerable number of the articles concerning Italian immigration were unfavorable to them, causing the deterioration of relations between the native born and the Italian immigrants. This retarded the immigrant's assimilation. See also John Hingham, *Strangers in the Land* (New York: Atheneum, 1963).

49. Whyte, p. 273.

come increasingly recognized. The Italian community is a group of people who follow a distinctive way of life or patterns of behavior that distinguish them from the people in the broader society to which they have come.[50] They are people who generally have come from the same place, most broadly from southern Italy, and beyond this there is often the similarity of region, province, and even town. They now are identified with a particular locality in the United States such as south Brooklyn or Paterson, where they now live or to which they have recently come. They speak the same language and often the same dialect, and share the same religion. They tend to stick together to help and support each other. They also have expectations of loyalty to one another. Alfredo, a machinist, told me forcefully, "The people here are all Italian . . . most from my paese . . . many seem to be envious of my advancement and often ask how I am able to do this and that. . . . The answer is that I try to do all things to improve. . . . Still I will never turn my back on my own. . . . I will help them whenever I can."[51]

The emphasis in Germani, Eisenstadt, and Gordon on the distinct social group that assimilates culturally while retaining its distinct social identity is another way of indicating the central role of the immigrant community.[52] It seemed as if these three distinguished scholars had given a private lecture on this point to Mario, who one evening, in his usually thoughtful manner, remarked, "I think the Italians who come, the immigrant, needs the tie with other immigrants and being with other Italians . . . their similar ways

---

50. Joseph Fitzpatrick, "The Importance of Community in the Process of Immigrant Assimilation," *IMR* (Fall 1966), pp. 5–16. See R. Breton, "Institutional Completeness of Ethnic Communities and the Personal Relations of Immigrants," *AJS* (September 1964); Andrew Greeley, *Why Can't They Be Like Us?* (New York: E. P. Dutton & Co., Inc., 1971), pp. 103–10.

51. Interview, Alfredo (machinist).

52. Gino Germani, "Migration and Acculturation," in Philip Hauser, ed., *Handbook for Social Research in Urban Areas* (UNESCO, 1965), pp. 159–78. See S. N. Eisenstadt, *The Absorption of Immigrants* (London: Routledge & Kegan Paul Ltd., 1954). Gordon, *Assimilation in American Life.*

and customs."[53] Indeed, if the immigrants are torn too rapidly from the traditional cultural framework of their lives and thrown too rapidly as strangers into a cultural environment that is unfamiliar, the danger of social disorganization is very great. The Italian immigrants need the traditional social group in which they are at home, in which they find their psychological satisfaction and security, in order to move with greater confidence toward greater interaction with the larger society.

The impact of the elements of the community on its members is in the conscious sharing of common ends, norms, and means, which gives the group an awareness of the bonds of membership that constitute their unity.[54] Antonio, a natural comedian, in one of his rare moments of seriousness expressed it in this manner, "I like living here in this neighborhood. . . . I feel close to the others (Italians) . . . and that life which I love."[55] The bearded Gaetano described it this way, "The people are good. . . . I feel good here (in the social center) with them. Here in the United States it is all work; there is no way to enjoy life . . . there is no pleasure in life. Americans don't seem to enjoy life. . . . Even if they do go out they always talk about money or their job. . . . In Italy you come home from work, eat a large meal with the family, relax, go back to work, come home again to the family. . . . After dinner you go out with them for a nice passeggiata (stroll). . . . Here (neighborhod) I feel I am with my own."[56] In both instances one sees a sharing of certain norms and ends that help to delineate the Italian community.

Interaction as a primary group is also required, and this generally cannot take place at too great a distance from the larger society. This can be illustrated by the case of Gianfranco. Even with the base of security of the ethnic enclave,

53. Interview, Mario (lawyer).
54. Fitzpatrick, p. 9.
55. Interview, Antonio (electrician).
56. Interview, Gaetano (dye-house worker).

this quiet, scholarly, almost ascetic-looking young Italian immigrant seemed overwhelmed at being in America. His expression was one of painful confusion. On one occasion he got up enough courage to apply personally for admission to a college, since he had been a university student before coming to the United States. He apparently was rudely rebuffed by a secretary who saw his difficulty with the language and concluded that he was unqualified for admission. A year had passed since the incident and the respondent still showed the signs of deep hurt over this encounter as he conveyed the story to me. Some of his fellow townsmen learned of this and confronted him. One in particular, with a greater facility with the language, encouraged him to make another attempt, and together they made another foray on the larger society. On this rather simple level one can see the kind of reinforcement the immigrant derives from life in the enclave.

In the case of the Italian immigrants, the active reality that is the community is not the larger society but the Italian subculture of the larger society.[57] The basic area limits are necessary to define community. Gans was able to locate various subcultures according to different attitudes and values. Gans states,

> The basis of adult life is peer group sociability. . . . Membership in the group is based primarily on kinship. As already noted, brothers, sisters, and cousins of the husband and wife—and their spouses—are at the core.[58]

Godparents and single individuals are also included, and perhaps neighbors. Those included are relatively compatible in terms of background, interests, and attitudes. Gans links community with a number of institutions, such as the church, parochial school, formal school, political and civic groups, and businesses.[59] According to him,

57. Fitzpatrick, p. 9.
58. Gans, p. 74.
59. *Ibid.*

these institutions—predominantly Italian—exist outside the peer group society, but are linked with it if and when they can be used to meet group and individual needs.[60]

These constitute the community since they are an accepted part of the life of the people and their functions are often "an auxiliary of those of the peer society."[61] Gans uses *community* in the social sense, describing the set of institutions that are dealt with by the peer-group society. Though located in the neighborhood, their functions have little to do with it. "For this reason the role of the institutions . . . can be described almost without reference to the spatial community or neighborhood."[62] Thus a major index of community is a knowledge of the neighborhood and those aspects which are the tangible points of identity. A church, a store, a club, a street corner, a place of work are such points of identity, since they are the spatial context for the social life of a group of people. Many of the Italian respondents knew each other on a number of different levels. In each case some aspect of the community brought the immigrants together. For Father Tomaso and Donato it was the church, while for Bruno it was the local club across from his home: "There I have many friends . . . they speak the same dialect. Most of use are mad for soccer and opera."[63] Michelle associated with the local store, which was well stocked with Italian specialties. Gaetano identified with the local social center, where he ran an Italian bar, a replica of its counterpart in Salerno.

The immigrant community serves as a kind of staging area, a beachhead where Italian immigrants can remain until they absorb new ideas and habits that make possible their adjustment to an alien environment. The ethnic community as a buffer fulfills a vitally important function both to the

60. *Ibid.*, p. 105.
61. Fitzpatrick, p. 13.
62. Gans, p. 104.
63. Interview, Bruno (unskilled worker).

newcomer and to the receiving society.[64] As Marcello said, "Here I'm familiar with the customs, since most who live in the neighborhood are Italian. Many of my friends helped me, since they spoke Italian and knew English. I wanted to go back as soon as I came here, but I adjusted to a different way of life. . . . I found a good way of life."[65] After six years of residence in an Italian neighborhood, Alfredo could say with confidence that he wanted to move.

The relative stability of residence patterns in the Italian neighborhood becomes more apparent as we take a closer view of the three-generational span. Among the first-generation respondents the average length of residence in the present neighborhood was 8.1 years. Paul was typical of most of them as he described his movement. "I came here four years ago from South Brooklyn. That was an all-Italian area with many immigrants. It was an old . . . very old area . . .; the housing was not good . . . and the surroundings were very depressing, especially on a cold winter night. I wanted a nicer home and was able to afford a better apartment . . . so I came here."[66] Most of the first-generation respondents spent a considerable length of time in their previous neighborhood and the movement to their present residence represented the first major move of any kind. Most of them came from exclusively Italian neighborhoods, as had Paul along with many Italian immigrants and Italian-Americans, with other groups on the fringes like the Irish or Blacks. Paul the bright-eyed college student looked to the composition of the neighborhood and declared, "I prefer a mixed neighborhood like this."[67] In reality the neighborhood was not mixed with other groups, nor was his building.

In most cases the movement out of their previous residence was in part owing to a better economic situation at

---

64. Florence Kluckholm, "Family Diagnosis: Variations in the Basic Values of Family Systems," *Social Casework* (March 1958), pp. 63–73.
65. Interview, Marcello (insurance sales).
66. Questions 4 and 5, interview schedule. Interview, Paul.
67. *Ibid.*

home. For Mario, a lawyer, however, movement out would be an act of disgust and frustration. "If I change my residence it would not be tied to a search for social status . . . ; that is not very important to me. The think that may help me to decide to move is the future success of our local candidate, an Italian who is of and for the community and who is trying to unite the Italians politically. If he fails I may just move. . . . He's a good man but it's an uphill battle."[68] Bob, a moustachioed and modly dressed young man, is representative of the friendship patterns of the first-generation respondents. "At one time my friends were strictly Italian; . . . now I have a variety of friends . . . ; a number of really close ones are Jewish . . . but if I had to total them up and give a number I would have to admit the majority are Italian."[69] Most of the mixture among the friends of the respondents was on the professional or business level, with the most intimate relationships still confined to Italian-Americans.

Among the second-generation respondents there was very little variation in either their residence or friendship patterns.[70] The average residence of 13 years in the present neighborhood illustrated the relative stability of second-generation respondents as compared with that of the first. For most Italian-American respondents, the movement out came after many years in their previous neighborhood. Movement to their present residence was the first major break from the neighborhood for the first- and second-generation respondents. There was no major projection of future movement. The neighborhood of the second-generation Italian-Americans was predominantly Italian, with little real mixture. Many were like Lou, who put it simply, "I like it here . . . I'm comfortable here."[71] Sal, on the other hand,

---

68. Interview, Mario.
69. Interview, Bob (printer).
70. A. Gordon Darroch and Wilfred Marsten, "Ethnic Differentiation: Ecological Aspects of a Multidimensional Concept," *IMR* (Fall 1969), pp. 71–93.
71. Interview, Lou.

perceived that he was in a mixed neighborhood and reaffirmed his closeness to his Italian past: "I like the neighborhood I'm in . . . ; it has different kinds of people but I
never forget or turn my back on being Italian . . . it's too
much a part of me."[72] Still others reveal an inner conflict
of loyalties, like Larry, whose usual infectious grin now
turned into a serious expression as he declared, "I prefer
an Italian neighborhod, but I came into conflict with my
fiancée, who is Italian herself but has different ideas. To
some extent I see her point, since you can't experience all
ways of life, different ones, in an all-Italian neighborhood.
Whatever we do I will always want to see and want to help
my own kind to get to a better level of life no matter where
I am."[73] While there is some evidence of more mixture
among friends, still the predominant ones, the more social
ones, were with Italian-Americans. Four of five of the second-
generation respondents expressed a desire to live in a mixed
neighborhood but were in reality living in one that was
Italian-American.

Of the third-generation Italian-American respondents, the
average length of residence in the present neighborhood was
14.2 years. In many respects the pattern was similar to that
of the first- and second-generation respondents. Most came
from heavily Italian-American areas and were currently living in similar ones, with only one major exception. There
was a greater mixture with other ethnic groups either within the neighborhood or in the actual dwelling. The mixture
is often with the Irish or Jewish. All third-generation respondents showed a greater disposition to live in a mixed
neighborhood and, like Vincent, affirmed, "where I live
makes no difference . . . ; this can hardly be called an Italian
neighborhood."[74] Individual dwellings and the neighborhoods still had strong Italian-American representation.

72. Interview, Sal (undertaker).
73. Interview, Larry (auto dealer).
74. Interview, Vincent (student).

There is greater evidence of mixture in the friendship patterns of the third-generation respondents, however; many of the more intimate friendships were with other Italian-Americans. Members of the immediate or extended family moved with many of the third-generation respondents, many of whom lived in the same building or neighborhood.

In another sense the residential patterns of Italians can be seen as an element in their assimilation and an indicator of other elements of assimilation.[75] Residential segregation has an important impact on other aspects of their assimilation.[76] It is a factor in highlighting differences between groups by making such groups more visible. It also enables the ethnic group, the Italian in this case, to hold on to its peculiar traits and group structure. The more the Italians are physically isolated from the host society, the greater their tendency to maintain links with Italy.[77] The residential patterns uncovered in the previous pages would seem to indicate that those living in areas with high concentrations of other Italians would be less well assimilated than those who live in nonsegregated areas.

The ethnic group has a special relationship to the social structure.

within the ethnic group there develops a network of organizations and informal social relationships which permit and encourage the members of the ethnic group to remain within the confines of the group for all of their primary relationships and some of their secondary relationships throughout all the stages of the life cycle.[78]

Herbert Gans found that working-class Italian-Americans tended to confine their meaningful social and institutional participation to other working-class Italian-Americans,

---

75. Otis Duncan and Stan Lieberson, "Ethnic Segregation and Assimilation," *American Journal of Sociology* (January 1959), pp. 364–74.

76. I will discuss these other aspects of assimilation in chapter 3.

77. Stan Lieberson, "The Impact of Residential Segregation on Ethnic Assimilation," *Social Forces* (October 1961) pp. 52–57.

78. Gordon, p. 34.

mostly to the same generation and the same neighborhood.[79]
Culturally he found few traces of the immigrant way of life
in these American-born semi-skilled and unskilled workers.
I found that even when the Italian language was retained,
it was not spoken fluently. Most second-generation respondents could not read Italian. All of the immigrant and first-
generation respondents could speak and read Italian.[80] By
the third generation I found a total absence of ability either
to speak or read the language. Most of the respondents in
all three groups, however, felt that they would like to see
their children speak the language. Gans's subjects retained
their particular dialect as a second language, although their
own children, the third generation, are not being taught
the language and will grow up knowing only English.[81] All
three groups of the Italian-Americans still preferred Italian
cooking. While the structural pattern of the "peer group
society" is in many ways compatible with their ancestral
Italian social patterns, this emphasis on peer-group soci-
ability is a general working-class cultural pattern and not
peculiarly Italian. Thus, a number of stimuli and predispositions have served to perpetuate an Italian-American
subsociety.

---

79. Gans, p. 13.
80. Segregation and the ability to speak English are in part a function of
length of residence. But the persistence of this association is evident even
after length of residence is considered.
81. Gans's study is in many respects lacking, and the subtitle *Group and
Class in the Life of Italian-Americans* is misleading and inaccurate in that he
proposes that his sample of West Enders was almost, but not entirely representative of second-generation Italian-American life. Gans's book is a study
of working-class Italian-Americans and is not reflective of an overall subsocietal way of life. But even with this cautionary note, many of his conclusions are based on myths, which he then perpetuates. These include the
following: that the social and economic conditions that existed in Southern
Italy are still in existence today; southern Italian parents had little or no
interest in their children; all people outside the family are looked upon as
strangers. Gans does not possess an intimate knowledge of southern-Italian
culture. Moreover, what he fails to take into account is that the behavior of
his subjects may have its roots not in Italy but in the American ghetto and
slum. Perhaps the will to succeed and achieve, which was so strong in Italy
as to bring southern Italians to the United States in large numbers, may
have been affected by a set of conditions peculiarly American.

Conclusion

Both the Italian immigrant and the Italian-American are urban residents. Ninety-one point eight percent of all Italians reside in urban areas and 69.3% live in the Northeastern region.

The Italian immigrants of today are not so handicapped as their forebears in coping with an urban environment. Southern Italy is no longer a peasant society. Increased urbanization and industrialization have resulted in the destruction of the old rural culture. Hence, the southern Italian immigrants arrive with something of an urban outlook. The Italian immigration of today is part of a rural-to-urban flow underway in Italy. Despite the destruction of the rural values, the southern Italian immigrant has not had time to develop or absorb new ones. Hence, he is still ill equipped to cope with urban living. Nearly half of our immigrant respondents were born in communities of 5,000 or less. In overall outlook and occupation they are unprepared to take their place in an automated society.

The Italian enclave is formed as a result of past immigration patterns, family link immigration, and outgroup rejection. The family-link type of immigration illustrates the importance of the family to Italian society. This type of immigration is influential in the formation of the enclave and its persistence. The Italian subsociety serves as a source of security and satisfaction for the Italian immigrants and Italian-Americans. The Italian subsociety has a distinctive way of life, which marks it off from the broader society. In it there is the similarity of language, customs, religion, values, and norms. The conscious sharing of these elements gives the group an awareness of itself and its unity. The subsociety is also characterized by interaction on the primary and secondary levels. The Italian community serves as a kind of staging area where Italians remain, absorbing new ideas, values, and the like, which make possible their adjustment to an alien and urban environment.

As one moves along the three-generational span among Italian-Americans, the size of the city of birth and of current residence increases. My findings suggest the greatest physical mobility between the first to the second generation. In particular there is residential stability among the second- and third-generation respondents. If the Italians move, it is often within the current city environment.

The residential patterns of both the Italian immigrants and Italian-Americans are altered as a result of their movement into the higher socioeconomic categories and increased outgroup acceptance. My findings would suggest that residential patterns are changed on this basis, but I have suggested that a structural separation may result in the persistence of the Italian subsociety.[82]

---

82. These assumptions will be explored in chapters 3 and 7.

2
Familism, Social Structure, and Urbanization

The ethos of familism is a response to certain stimuli features coming from the social structure of southern Italy. It may be thought of as a set of ideas that express, evaluate, and rationalize the organization of south Italian rural society. Familism as a descriptive construct refers to a pervasive psychic interest and cultural value that arise from the family system. As a cultural characteristic of the south Italian social structure, it is internalized in the individual personality. What develops is a cultural disposition of southern Italian society and the personal predisposition of southern Italians.

Familism as a predisposition is brought with the south Italian when he emigrates to America. This predisposition is subject to the stimuli emanating from a new urban environment and a new social structure. The rural southern Italian coming to an urban America will undergo a number of changes in his family structure. The length of urban residence of rural southern Italians and its intergenerational mobility will be related to less immediate family participation, fewer extended family relationships, and greater extrafamilial social relations. This will result in a changed political outlook by subsequent generations of Italian-Americans.

Edward Banfield in a study of a South Italian community, described "Montegrano" as a social system that lacks moral sanctions outside of the immediate family. The Montegranesi are pictured as opposed to any meaningful association outside the nuclear family. They are unwilling to engage in any political problem or activity in the interest of the community. Moreover, they are unable to achieve and maintain formal organizations. He suggests that the Montegranesi behave always as if they were following the rule of amoral familism. They act to:

> maximize the material short run advantage of the nuclear family; assume that all others will do likewise.[1]

This rule becomes the dominant ethos of Montegrano, and the nuclear family is the dominant social unit. What follows is the absence of corporate groups or informal stable group alliances between the nuclear family and the community. Community leaders are few in number, and political alignments remain temporary and contingent.

While Banfield's ideas still retain a core of validity, they must be modified. According to Silverman:

> Extrafamilial ties are not lacking, but those that exist (friendships, patronage relationships, casual groupings, etc.) are shifting, informal, and dyadic. Moreover, political action (as reflected in voting behavior, political machines, and the like) is regular and explicable, though it is flexible and lends itself readily to realignment.[2]

---

1. Edward Banfield, *The Moral Basis of a Backward Society* (Glencoe, Ill.: The Free Press, 1958) , p. 83.
2. Sydel Silverman, "Amoral Familism Reconsidered," *American Anthropologist* 70 (February 1964) : 3. See Pier Giovanni Grasso, *Personalita Gio-*

Ethos is not an adequate explanation of behavior. There are the realistic conditions of overpopulation, underemployment, land hunger, and so on. There are the external constraints of the state, which remove responsibility at the local level, impose restrictive regulations on voluntary organization, and leave powers to officials and those with influence. The Italians then often see politics and political action as hopeless. Community is a weak structural unit.[3] Banfield's basic insight was essentially correct but it is not ethos which is the cause of the nuclear family as the dominant social unit. In other words his explanation is backwards.

> it is not the ethos of "amoral familism" that is the cause of these characteristics of the social system, but they are the basis of the ethos.[4]

All fifteen of the immigrant respondents were acutely aware of the class system that existed in the communities in which they lived prior to coming to America. As Mina, a student, described it, "Italian society is divided by social class. The class you're in determines how people treat you, your friends, other relationships and even your opportunities."[5]

From the responses of the immigrant respondents emerged descriptions of the patterns of social stratification in southern Italy. The social structure of southern Italian society is characterized by four strata: *galantuomini* (upper class), *artigiani-mercanti* (artisans and merchants), *contadini* (peasants), and *giornalieri* (day laborers). The *Galantuomo* class usually consists of large landowners who are often absentee owners. Also included in this class are the professional people such as doctors, lawyers, teachers, and bureaucrats. These members of the galantuomo class in the past have

---

vaniti in Tranzione: Dal Familismo al Personalismo (Zurich: Pas Verlag, 1964).

3. The term comunità in Italian stands not for national or public mindedness, but for the community that exists in the monastery.
4. Silverman, "Amoral Familism Reconsidered," p. 3.
5. Interview, Mina (student).

been able to do little to counterbalance the power of the landed gentry. They too were economically dependent upon them. The artisan is dependent for his living upon both the peasant and the upper class. While the artisan may be only a little better off than the contadino, he is socially removed from him. The contadini have title to small portions of land and usually have a modest house in the town. They often own implements and animals. The giornaliero class are propertyless agricultural day laborers and the lowest stratum of south Italian society.[6] Though the difference materially or in standard of living may not be great socially, there is a barrier between them.

Eight of the fifteen immigrant respondents came from the same coastal town, where farming and fishing predominated. The town, perched high on a hill overlooking the Adriatic, winds upward to different gradations. As Alfredo put it, "The class distinctions are very great. It even determines where you live."[7] The people who live at the different gradations conform to the overall class structure of the community. The lowest stratum resides at the lower gradation while those of the upper stratum live at the upper gradation. The upper-class residents regard themselves as being superior and more civilized than those down below. The lower classes regard those above as parasites and thieves. They do not regard the upper town residents as superior. According to Gaetano, "I never felt inferior to them. They got there not by their own intelligence. In reality they may really be inferior to me."[8]

What emerges from this description is a portrait of a class system that is disjunctive and one in which the strata tend toward closure. The disjunctive nature of the rural stratifi-

6. Leonard Moss and Stephen Cappannari, "Estate and Class in a South Italian Hill Village," *American Anthropologist* (April 1962), pp. 287–300. See also Sydel Silverman, "An Ethnographic Approach to Social Stratification: Prestige in a Central Italian Community," *American Anthropologist* (August 1966), pp. 899–921.

7. Questions 3, 36–42, interview schedule. Interview, Alfredo (machinist).

8. Interview, Gaetano (dye-house worker).

cation system is seen most clearly at the upper and lower strata. Social contacts between the upper echelon and all others in the community are limited by prescribed patterns of behavior. According to Gaetano, "To advance, one must be born into the family of middle or upper class."[9] Another indication of the closed nature of the social system are the patterns of marriage and occupations. Rarely does one marry out of his own social class. Occupations are often handed down from previous generations.

Luigi Barzini has said of the Italian family:

> Scholars have always recognized the Italian family as the only fundamental institution in the country, a spontaneous creation of the national genius, adapted throughout the centuries to changing conditions, the real foundation of whichever social order prevails. In fact, the law, the State and society function only if they do not directly interfere with the family's supreme interests.[10]

For a variety of historical reasons the societal organization in Italy has been relegated to a secondary position beneath the family.[11] As Polizzi notes:

> It appears through default of an incomplete feudal order or tradition and the many historical upsets, the southern Italian rural social structure . . . was atomized, and the kinship system came to prevail over other forms of organization as the central social referent.[12]

To the southern Italian, family still means not only husband and wife and children but also grandparents, uncles, cousins, and godparents, in short all blood and in-law relatives. In any southern Italian community, one can observe several or more family units. However, while the strongest bonds are within the nuclear family, the links with the ex-

---

9. *Ibid.*

10. Luigi Barzini, *The Italians* (New York: Atheneum, 1965) , p. 190.

11. These factors will be considered in chapter 4.

12. Anthony Polizzi, "Southern Italy: Its Peasantry and Change" (doctoral dissertation, Cornell University, 1958) , p. 22.

tended family are firm indeed.[13] "Family solidarity" gives
the family its essential unity and cohesiveness. The behavior
of one member of the family is often something that concerns all family members. As Covello writes:

> The family solidarity was manifested by uniformity of be-
> havior, adherence to family tradition and, also a community
> of economic interests.[14]

Barzini has noted the role of the family in Italian society,
as follows:

> The Italian family is a stronghold in a hostile land; within
> its walls and among its members, the individual finds conso-
> lation, help, advice, provision, loans, weapons, allies and ac-
> complices to aid in his pursuits. No Italian who has a family
> is ever alone. He finds in it refuge in which to lick his wounds
> after a defeat, or an arsenal and a staff for his victorious
> drives.[15]

In the past the lack of secondary group structures gave the
family a "functional autonomy" that was in keeping with
its position in the larger society.[16]

The southern Italian family is father dominated but
mother centered. Polizzi suggests that the family might be
better viewed as pyramidal. However, he notes, "the potential power of the father is often seriously lessened by the
social emotional leadership of the mother."[17] The role of
the wife is one of primary concern with the private life of
the family, while the public role is the father's province.

---

13. For interesting treatments of family and relationships in the Italian-
American novel, see Jerre Mangione, *Mount Allegro* (Boston: Houghton,
Mifflin & Co., 1943).

14. Leonard Covello, *The Social Background of the Italo-American School
Child* (Leyden: E. J. Brill, 1967).

15. Barzini, p. 190.

16. Banfield, pp. 103–20.

17. Polizzi, p. 71. See also Leonard Moss and Walter Thompson, "The
South Italian Family: Literature and Observation," *Human Organization*
(Spring 1959); Aubrey Menen, "The Italian Family is a Commune," *New
York Times Magazine* (March 1, 1970).

While this separation has been maintained in the past, one wonders what impact the changed status of women in the family will have as they enter the sphere of work outside the family. Many changes can be expected to increase the areas of strain.

While children are an integral part of the family it is still adult centered. It is misleading to think that a "seen and not heard" philosophy dominates the south Italian family. Regarding the role of children in the family, Polizzi writes:

> The child in southern Italian peasant society is not conceived of as someone whose inherent makeup necessitate that he be sheltered and nurtured in a separate existence. . . . Only infrequently is he left out of adult gatherings . . . his early socialization is rather informally shared among several village "agents" both inside and outside the nuclear family unit. . . ."[18]

The rural southern Italian family in contrast to the urban family is a "productive consumptive unit." Perceptions of the outside world are sifted through an "economic filter." "An economic interpretation of reality" Polizzi concludes, is pervasive and is reflected in "practically every sphere of southern Italian life."[19]

Covello has noted that the similarity of his respondents in all dimensions indicated a social structure in which communal norms were so powerful that individual reactions were part of the traditional reactions of the community.

> There was little need for the individual to assert himself; all his activities, all his thoughts, were prescribed by a traditional set of folkways, mores, customs.[20]

Having the family as the center of the individual member's loyalty made it difficult to develop a social outlook that went

18. Polizzi's description of the southern-Italian family is in contrast to that of Herbert Gans. See Gans, pp. 45–73.
19. *Ibid.*, p. 76.
20. Covello, p. 159.

beyond that of the family.[21] The importance of this factor
to the development of community interests is noted by Covello:

> The social training of the young people, therefore, was di-
> rected toward a sharp discrimination between the family to
> which one must pay all kinds of allegiance, and the other
> families of the community itself which consisted of strangers
> and, as such, were due no special consideration. . . . A demarca-
> tion line was always drawn between the home and the com-
> munity, and allegiance to one's family was made to appear
> more significant, more imperative, than allegiance to groups
> larger than the family.[22]

The ethos of amoral familism then may be seen as emerging out of southern Italian social patterns. To the extent
that moral sanctions are lacking in relation to persons outside the nuclear family, is a reflection of the scarcity of lasting extrafamilial ties. Other aspects of the amoral ethos are
also expressions of Southern social organization: the mistrust of persons outside the immediate family, the skeptical
attitude toward cooperation, and the like. Also closely related is a general apprehensiveness toward the world and
the future and a feeling of helplessness about one's ability
to control the environment.

In southern Italy urbanity is a central value; the city is
ultimately the source of all that is most highly prized in
the society as a whole. Urbanity implies civilization.[23] Towns
and villages replicate in miniature the culture patterns of
the city. All members of the Southern community—elite,
petty landowner, and landless cultivator—play out the major
part of their lives in an urban-like agglomerate. Even the

---

21. I have noted previously that with immigration to the U. S. the Italian
subsociety is formed and perpetuated. With this comes the development of a
community concept that was imperfectly developed while in Italy.

22. Covello, p. 162. See also Banfield, pp. 103–20; Grasso, p. 221. Grasso
argues that a conscious attempt must be made to move from familism to
personalism, a distinctive personalism characterized by the solidarity that
arises out of collaboration for the good of the community.

23. Polizzi, p. 44.

lowest strata are directly involved in town life, even though their participation in some areas of it may be limited. In the south each individual or small family aspires to emulate ever more closely the "civilized," urbane ideals of the society. This is the motive for the petty peasant proprietor's becoming an inactive renter. Southern Italians are prisoners not of the ethos but of the social structure.

Familism then emerges as a key construct.[24] In one sense it refers to a kind of central pervasive psychic interest and cultural value emanative from the family system. The relative individuality of southern Italians develops out of and is sustained by their essentially familistic orientation. Familism may be viewed as a cultural characteristic of southern Italian social structure, which is internalized in the individual personality.[25]

The modernization of Italy—its urbanization and industrialization, the impact of the media, and the wider transportation network linking all of Italy—is creating within the southern Italian family in particular certain centripetal forces similar to the ones created on arrival in the United States. Many of the younger members of the family, male and female, are leaving home to go to the university or to seek opportunity in the city. All of these forces are producing loyalties competing with that to the family by developing allegiances to other social institutions.[26] No longer is one's social outlook confined to the village. Many have traveled not only to the provincial capitals but to other urban centers. Thousands in search of seasonal employment in the industrial centers of Europe return with an altered social outlook.[27]

Many young people develop an active disdain for life in the village, which often leads to open ruptures in the nuclear family. A visit to the rural areas of Italy is the basis for

24. Questions 10–16, interview schedule.
25. Grasso.
26. Ibid.
27. Ibid.

dramatic evidence of this development, for there the population is largely made up of old people. The young have fled to the city. Umberto, a college student, described his family's situation in Italy. "My father owned a lot of land. He worked hard but never got anywhere. At the end of the year he spent as much as he earned. Many like my father complained that the laborers wanted too much. When you go to sell your crop the price goes up. Many in our town either sold their land or abandoned it. If I stayed there the only opportunity would be farming like my father. The city, though, has more opportunities for work and a better life."[28]

Increasingly, other members outside of the family are being accepted as friends with links of loyalty and obligation to them. The circle of friendships is widening to other towns and even regions. Traditionally, anyone outside the family group was viewed with indifference and, often, hostility. As Covello writes:

> Solidarity was comprehensible only within limits of familial existence; it did not apply to other aggregates. It is probably no exaggeration to say that la famiglia was the only social concept, and that any other terms such as paese . . . or villaggio, . . . had no other than a purely spatial connotation. It would be hard to find in southern Italy a synonym for the English word "community."[29]

Thus, the southern Italian is developing a wider, more modern social outlook, which must alter or change existing family relationships, however slight this may be at this particular moment in history.

The developments that I have noted have modified Banfield's findings. Even when we consider these modifications, the southern Italian family still remains as the basic psycho-social-economic unit that is the primary focus of the individual and that gives him status and security.[30]

---

28. Interview, Umberto (college student).
29. Covello, p. 152.
30. Polizzi, p. 44. See also Banfield.

Since the southern Italian family is undergoing some modification in Italy, what happens when the southern Italian family moves from an essentially rural environment to an urban one? Thirteen of our immigrant respondents indicated that their fathers were the principal decision-makers. That same number indicated that their fathers were the chief disciplinarians when decisions were made. Only three of the fifteen immigrants maintained that there was ever any extended discussion. Fourteen out of fifteen of the respondents showed little dissatisfaction or disagreement with the decision-making and disciplinary arrangement. This would seem to indicate that the family patterns remain relatively stable during the initial years of living in urban America. The southern Italian family gradually becomes less patriarchal as loyalties outside the home start to impinge upon its traditional role.[31] As Ianni notes:

> The adolescent children of these families in conflict in the past became the teenagers in conflict popularly identified with the Little Italies of the Twenties and Thirties. The street corner gangs made famous by William Foote Whyte emerged as teen-agers, no longer encompassed by an integrated and need-satisfying family, took to the street corners and peer group associations. The family had neither the means nor the living space to provide recreation to replace the labor previously expected of the adolescent. New conflicts also appeared in the parent-child relationship as the teenager attempted to transmit his newly acquired American expectations of life into the weakened family structure.[32]

Four of the five first-generation respondents held that their fathers were the principal decision-makers in their family. This same number indicated that their mothers were increasingly consulted on a variety of matters, but there was little discussion with the other members of the family. Four of the five first-generation respondents ex-

31. Vincenzo Cezareo, "Immigrati e associaciazionismi voluntaria," *Studi Emigrazioni* (October 1966), pp. 29–50.

32. Francis Ianni, "The Italo American Teen Ager," *The Annals* (November 1961), p. 74.

pressed strong disagreement with this arrangement. The female members of the first-generation family are increasingly provided with formal education as well as family education for marriage. The son is expected to work hard and to contribute to the family income. The rights of the individual member of the family are increasingly recognized; however, not as much as desired in some cases. These are indications that the father is starting to lose his primary status in the family; while the mother is still the center of domestic life, work outside the family gives her more importance and independence.[33]

The first-generation family is in transition, disorganized, and in conflict, and the family culture is in question. Children in the first-generation Italian family become increasingly independent of the family as a result of outside employment.[34] The position of the family is further aggravated by the loss of that strong family culture which had been an indispensable part of their unity in Italy. While Italian culture is transmitted only by the family, the American culture is transmitted by American institutions other than the family.[35]

Four of the five second-generation respondents asserted that there was shared decision-making with the other members of the family. Discipline was shared between mother and father. Individual members of the family often shape their own goals in life as a result of their increased independence. There are many signs of the subordination of the family to the individual. Female members of the family are educated with reference to personality development rather than to future marriage.[36] The son is expected to

33. Paul Campisi, "Ethnic Family Patterns: The Italian Family in the United States," *AJS* 53 (1948) : 434–47.

34. Bartolomeo Palisi, "Patterns of Social Participation in a Two Generation Sample of Italian Americans," *Sociological Quarterly* (Spring, 1966), pp. 167–78. See also George Psathas, "Ethnicity, Social Class and Adolescent Independence from Parental Control," *ASR* (August 1957), pp. 415–23.

35. *Ibid.*

36. Campisi, pp. 444–49. See also Gans, *The Urban Villiager* (New York: The Free Press, 1962), pp. 54–73.

acquire an education. The mother's role is also altered in that her independence from the family is not only in the form of work, but in an increased social life apart from it. The second-generation family moves further from the traditional Italian pattern, but does not abandon it entirely.[37]

Four of the five third-generation respondents indicated that their fathers and mothers shared decision-making and disciplinary roles. There was more room for disagreement and children were regularly consulted. There was also greater evidence of satisfaction with this arrangement than in the other generational groupings. The third-generation family tends to be urban, democratic, and modern. In-group solidarity decreases compared to the first- and second-generation families. The functions of the third-generation family are limited primarily to affectional.

We may also obtain an understanding of the impact of the urban environment on the Italian family by looking at family size, and immediate and extrafamilial participation.

The immediate family of the Italian immigrant respondents tended to be larger than that of the first, second, and third generations.[38] The immediate family size of the immigrant respondents was 6, while that of the first generation was 5.4; second-generation family size was 3.3; the size of the third-generation family was 4.4.

In addition, immediate family participation is higher for the first generation than for the second generation.[39] It is interesting to note that five of the seven Italian immigrant respondents who had parents living in the United States were also living in the same neighborhood. Twelve of the

37. Francis Ianni, "Residential and Occupational Mobility as Indices of the Acculturation of an Ethnic Group," *Social Forces* (October, 1957), pp. 65–72. See also idem, "The Italo-American Teen Ager," p. 75.

38. Bartolomeo J. Palisi, "Ethnic Generation and Family Structure," *Journal of Marriage and the Family* (February 1966), p. 50. Palisi found the immediate family of first-generation Italian-Americans to be smaller than that of the second generation. See also Gans, pp. 45–46.

39. *Ibid.* On this point Palisi's findings are in conformity with mine.

fifteen immigrant respondents had a member of the extended family either in the neighborhood or the same city. Four of five of the first-generation respondents had their parents living in the same neighborhood.[40] All of those of the first generation had a member of the extended family either in the same town or neighborhood. Three of the five second-generation respondents lived in the same neighborhood as their parents. All five had a member of the extended family in the same town or neighborhood. The relative stability of this pattern is seen in the third generation, where four of the five respondents had their parents and a member of the extended family living in the same neighborhood, or at least living in the same town.

Members of the first generation lived in closer physical proximity than did those of either the second or third generation. If we consider visiting patterns on a per week basis, the second-generation and third-generation respondents visited relatives and were in turn visited more frequently than the first-generation or the immigrant respondents. These findings suggest that the second- and third-generation respondents become increasingly active outside the family as they acculturate to urban values, but at the same time retain family contacts.[40] The extended family plays a greater role for the second- and third-generation respondents than for those of the first.[41]

Conclusion

These findings show that the ethos of familism remains essentially valid today. I have asserted, however, that familism arises out of the social structure of southern Italian society. Class distinctions result in a clear demarcation of residence, occupation, friendships, extra-familial relation-

---

40. Questions 4b, 4c, interview schedule.
40. *Ibid.*
41. I shall discuss the political significance of a changed family structure in chapters 5 and 6.

ships, and dress. The social class system of southern Italy is essentially disjunctive and tends toward closure. There is little social contact between classes, particularly the upper and lower echelons.

The family for the southern Italian remains the supreme societal organization. The southern rural social structure was atomized and the kinship system came to dominate over forms of social organization. The family remains an important and essential referent for the southern Italian. It is father-dominated, as evidenced in his disciplinary and decision-making roles. The social system of southern Italy lacks moral sanctions outside of the immediate family. As a result, the southern Italian is unable to support community-wide interests and the community remains a weak structural unit. Familism as a cultural characteristic of southern Italian social structure is internalized and becomes a personal predisposition.

Familism is undergoing change in Italy because of the impact of the twin forces of urbanization and industrialization. Hence, the circle of friendships is widening, with the resultant development of new and competing loyalties.

The movement of rural southern Italians to an urban America produces changes in family decision-making and discipline. The major determinants are length of city residence and intergenerational mobility. As one moves from the first to the third generation, decision-making and discipline are shared. Members of the family become increasingly independent. Also, family size declines gradually with length of city residence and as members move along the generational span. Immediate family participation decreases from the first to the third generation, while extrafamilial participation increases.

3

The Structural Assimilation of Italian-Americans

The institutionalization of the behavior of Italian immigrants and Italian-Americans occurs within the American
social structure. From that structure flow certain stimuli in
the form of demands and expectations. Current images of
Italians, along with those from earlier periods, are institutionalized and interact significantly in producing demands
on and role expectations of Italians.

The process of integration of the Italian immigrant entails the learning of new roles, the transfer of primary group
values, and the extension of participation beyond the pri-
mary-group level. One demand of the core society is for the
complete renunciation of the Italian's culture in favor of
that held by the core society. There is also the view that
the Italian remains a foreigner. This tends to reinforce an
Italian identification on both an individual and group level.

The social and political structure of the United States
serves to exclude the Italian from certain roles and limits

him to others. The lack of a structural assimilation is evidenced in a greater occupational, educational, and residential differentiation from the core society. The Italian is structurally unassimilated since he is not completely accepted into the primary face-to-face relations of the host society.

While the family structure is being altered in the direction of increased extended family and extrafamilial relationships, a structural separation has operated to confine the principal ones to other Italians of the same social class. Thus, a structural separation results in the retention of a district social identity and the persistence of an Italian subsociety.

Eisenstadt makes a distinction between cultural assimilation (acculturation), which refers to the major patterns, values, and roles of the society, and social assimilation, which is concerned with social participation.[1] The dichotomy between social and cultural assimilation is upheld by Gans. While cultural assimilation took place rapidly among the West End Italians, social assimilation did not take, and has not taken, place.[2] The institutions of the larger society have never been the channels of social assimilation.[3] Gordon focuses on the nature and structure of group life, maintaining that adequate analytical theory required that a distinc-

---

1. S. N. Eisenstadt, *The Absorption of Immigrants* (London: Routledge & Kegan Paul Ltd., 1954). Eisenstadt makes a distinction between types of roles or values in a society. Three are noted: universal, specialties, and alternatives. A pluralist society demands complete fulfillment of the first only, allows the emergence of a particularist immigrant body within the general social structure with special roles allocated to it and a limitation on the scope of alternatives to it. The immigrants are acculturated to the degree that they internalize and express the major American patterns and values, and fulfill the universal roles of the society. They are permitted to retain certain particularistic traits from their native culture. Cultural assimilation does not demand complete uniformity.

2. Herbert Gans, *The Urban Villagers* (New York: The Free Press, 1962), pp. 34–35.

3. Nathan Glazer and Daniel Moynihan, *Beyond the Melting Pot* (Cambridge, Mass.: MIT Press, 1963). This study in many ways supports Eisenstadt and Gans. They contend that depending on the length of residence, the ethnic group finds opportunities for social life. For the Jew and Italian the channels for social contact outside the group are still limited.

tion be made between structure and behavior in dealing with ethnic group adjustment.[4] The United States, according to Gordon, is a multiple melting-pot in which acculturation for all groups beyond the first generation of immigrants, without eliminating all value conflict, has been massive and decisive, but in which structural separation on the basis of race and religion emerges. This structural pluralism or separation of ethnic groups is brought about because of the prejudice of the majority group and partly because an insufficient number of the members of minority groups have wanted assimilation.[5]

The distinction made by Gordon between cultural and structural assimilation has the same implication as that of Eisenstadt, in that they are concerned with the same processes. By cultural assimilation Gordon means the adoption, by the immigrant, of those basic values and patterns of behavior of the host society which enable him to function effectively in the society.[6] By structural assimilation he means the complete acceptance of the immigrant into primary face-to-face relationships by the members of the host society. Cultural assimilation may and often does take place without the occurrence of structural assimilation.[7] Structural assimilation consists of many levels from participating in various types of occupations to intermarriage, which is the final stage of structural assimilation. In addition to these two assimilation variables, Gordon cites five others.[8] Once

4. Milton Gordon, *Assimilation in American Life* (New York: Oxford University Press, 1964), p. 131.

5. The presumed goal of cultural pluralism is to maintain enough subsocietal separation to see to the continuance of the ethnic cultural tradition and the existence of the group. The situation exists in which primary group contacts between those in ethnic groups are held to a minimum, even though secondary contacts on the job, etc., exist. Intimate primary group relations between those of different racial and religious groups remain at a minimum. Gordon, pp. 158-59.

6. Gordon, pp. 71-83.

7. Erich Rosenthal, "Acculturation Without Assimilation?: The Jewish Community of Chicago Illinois," *AJS* (November 1960), pp. 23-31.

8. Marital assimilation—large scale intermarriage.

Identificational assimilation—development of the sense of peoplehood based exclusively on the host society.

structural assimilation has occurred, either simultaneously with or subsequent to acculturation, all of the other types of assimilation will follow.[9]

When the Italian immigrant arrives in the United States he shares none of the common stock of memories, social traditions, and experiences that bind together those who were born in the host society. The principal variables that determine the actual process of assimilation are the immigrant's basic motivations and role expectations and the demands made upon him in the United States.[10] The immigrants interviewed revealed some level of frustration with Italian society, and an inability to achieve or fulfill their aspirations within it. Thus, a feeling of frustration and inadequacy motivates the Italian immigrant. The presence of an objective opportunity makes it possible to realize the desire to migrate. Like many of the immigrants interviewed, Gaetano and Gianfranco, prior to coming, viewed America as a land of opportunity. The former was originally excited about his decision to come, the latter came because of his father who became ill while in America. "Even though this is why I came I did expect a better life in America than in Italy."[11] As Eisenstadt observes,

The hope of resolving some of their frustrations in that country

Attitude receptional assimilation—absence of prejudice.
Behavior receptional assimilation—absence of discrimination.
Civic assimilation—absence of value and power conflict.
These seven variables will serve as the model for my discussion of assimilation of Italians.

9. Emilio Willens, "On the Concept of Assimilation," *American Anthropologist* (June 1955), p. 625. See also Gordon, p. 81; William Bernard, "The Integration of Immigrants in the United States," *IMR* (Spring 1967), pp. 23–31; M. C. McKenna, "Melting Pot: Comparative Observations in the U. S. and Canada," *Sociology and Social Research* (July 1969), pp. 443–47.

10. Jerold Heiss, "Factors Related to Immigrant Assimilation: Pre-Migration Traits," *Social Forces* (June 1969), pp. 422–28. See also Andrew Greeley, *Why Can't They Be Like Us?* (New York: E. P. Dutton & Co., Inc., 1971), pp. 53–59. Heiss hypothesized that the association between premigration traits and assimilation is owing to the association between premigration traits and abilitiy to learn a new culture. He concludes that "social integration in Italy is productive of these qualities of personality, and integration may also be 'caused' by them." See also Germani, pp. 167–73.

11. Interview, Gianfranco (bank clerk).

brings it within the scope of their perceptual field. These expectations may be more or less definite, and the images called up by the new country may differ widely as between one type of migrant and another.[12]

The Italian immigrant does develop expectations concerning his future role in American society. His motivation to leave Italy is not necessarily based on a sense of insecurity in every sphere of his life. In fact he may remain attached to his original society and culture. Thus, both the feeling of inadequacy and the consequent expectations in relation to the society may be limited to certain aspects of the total field of contact between him and his society. The Italian feels that certain instrumental goals, especially economic ones, cannot be attained within the institutional structure of Italian society.[13] As Mina candidly put it, "We came here for economic reasons, my father was a contadino. Before I came I thought the streets were paved with gold. I thought of beautiful buildings; . . . when I got here and saw the docks I was really shocked. There is opportunity here, but, it is up to the person to make it . . . he must take advantage of the opportunities."[14] Integration into American society may be delayed by the restriction of his expectation to only one or a few spheres of American life. The initial image he develops of America may be centered on one aspect of his frustration while, as regards the other aspects, he may still cling to Italian life.

When the Italian immigrant leaves Italy he detaches himself from all of the roles, social and political, he performed in Italy, and the range of his participation is restricted in America. His life is largely centered in primary membership groups, which further restricts his participation to only a few roles in the new society. With the old reference groups

12. Eisenstadt, p. 2. See also Mary Sengstock, "Differential Rates of Assimilation in an Ethnic Group: In Ritual, Social Interaction and Normative Culture." *IMR* (Spring 1969), pp. 18–30.

13. *Ibid.*, pp. 3–4.

14. Interview, Mina (student).

gone, a new set of images of America and Italy emerges.
Paolo explained it this way. "When I first came I didn't
see anything special . . . but one day I got lost on the subway in Manhattan. I never did comprehend the vastness of
city life and its diversity until then."[15] Arrival in the United
States means not only a limitation of the number or roles
and groups in which the Italian is active, but also a degree
of "desocialization."[16] According to Eisenstadt,

> the process . . . ultimately involves not only the attainment
> of specific goals or patterns of cultural gratification but also,
> and perhaps mainly, a resocialization of the individual, the
> reforming of his entire status image and set of values.[17]

The process of incorporation into American society may
be seen as the institutionalizing of Italians' role expectations.[18] The Italian immigrant faces immediate problems
of acquiring various skills. Giovanni recognized this when
he pointed out, like Mina, "Your opportunity is here, but
it depends on your work skills."[19] All of the immigrants interviewed stressed their difficulties with the language, which
served to limit their fulfilling their desired roles in the new
society. The Italian, to be sure, has to learn how to perform
new roles that are necessary in the new society. Gradually,
he has to rebuild and reform his idea of himself and his
status image by acquiring a new set of values and testing
it out in relation to the new roles not only available but
required of him. Alfredo's experience substantiates this conclusion. "I got my impression of America mostly from films.
I thought it was a great country in every respect. I took
four years of seamanship school but quit to come here. At
first my impression did not change. I wanted to go to West

---

15. Interview, Paolo (photographer).
16. Eisenstadt, p. 5.
17. *Ibid.*, p. 6.
18. Walter Zimmer, "Ethnic Assimilation and Corporate Group," *Sociological Quarterly* (Summer 1967), pp. 340–48.
19. Interview, Giovanni (unskilled laborer).

Point but I was delayed. I thought it would be much easier, but the language made it very difficult. I needed it for any advancement. It was not as easy as I had pictured it in Italy."[20] Eisenstadt's observation on this point is pertinent:

> The institutionalizing of roles can thus best be seen as a process of transformation of the immigrant's primary basic groups and fields of social relations—those groups which are the ground of his active participation in society. It is by the interweaving of these groups into the social structure of the receiving country that the immigrant's behavior becomes institutionalized, i.e., that his expectations become both compatible with the roles defined in the new society and capable of being realized in it.[21]

The process of integration for the Italian immigrant then entails the learning of new roles, the transformation of primary group values, and the extension of participation beyond the primary group in the main spheres of the social system.

Arrival in the United States is followed by two rather predictable patterns of reaction. The first is elation, followed by depression.[22] For most of the immigrants interviewed, elation lasted from arrival to one or two months. Following his decision to emigrate, the Italian experiences a good deal of anxiety, for he leaves the known for the unknown. As with Rafaello, the common way of reducing this anxiety is to reject any negative characteristics of the new country. Rafaello, the most recent immigrant interviewed, dwelt on the more positive aspects of his new environment. Thus, self-justification is one aspect of the elation pattern. For the Italian immigrant the initial situation contains an element of novelty that in turn provides the basis for a number of positive experiences. As Umberto explained it, "It was strange coming from a small town to a big city. It was a

---

20. Interview, Alfredo (machinist).
21. Eisenstadt, p. 7.
22. Alan Richardson, "A Psychological Study of Assimilation," *IMR* (Fall 1967), pp. 6–12.

big change for me."[23] For Umberto there is an element of fascination with his new surroundings. Thus, a certain novelty about the new situation forms the second component of the elation pattern. In the early days of his arrival the Italian senses greater social freedom since he has little opportunity to become involved with others and thus develops few obligations to others around him. He is able to assert a certain amount of ignorance of the new culture, which provides an even greater field of social freedom. This latter characteristic forms the third component of the elation pattern.[24]

Following six months to one year of residence, there is a discernible depression pattern among the Italian immigrants, revealing a lowering of the satisfaction level. When the novelty of the situation is gone, the Italian realizes the difference between the Italian and American societies. Antonio told me ruefully, "When I got here I had no friends. The language was very strange. I was really depressed. I was told opportunities were here."[25] The immigrant's new environment is not just new but very different from the one he left in Italy. The recognition of the difference often leads to an increased awareness of Italy. At every opportunity the Italian finds himself talking about his life in Italy. His nostalgic excursions often lead to an idealization of his former home. Most of the immigrants interviewed felt that they would like to spend the rest of their life in the United States.[26] But asked if they were satisfied with that life, only four out of fifteen offered a firm "yes." When confronted with a hypothetical situation of moving to Italy if they

---

23. Interview, Umberto (college student) .
24. Richardson, pp. 6–12.
25. Interview, Antonio (electrician) .
26. The following was used as an index of satisfaction:
    Question #69. Would you like to spend the rest of your life in the U. S.?
    Question #69a. Are you satisfied with your life in the U. S.?
    Question #70. Suppose you could live in Italy as well as you live here. Would you want to go back?

could live as well as they do in the United States, only three of the fifteen immigrants said they would not make the move to Italy, while the large part of them were either uncertain or declared they would.

The institutionalization of the Italian immigrant's behavior takes place within the American social structure. Within that structure, certain expectations by the immigrants develop, and certain demands are made upon them. Of course, the Italian may want to change in certain ways so as to attain certain goals within the new society. The problem, however, is how far within the new society these aspirations are capable of being realized. Does the social and political structure exclude the Italian from certain roles, thereby limiting him to others? How many and what roles is he performing with the institutions, social groups, and various sectors of American society? Are pressures put upon the Italian to change some or all of the cultural habits he may wish to retain?

Nonacceptance by the host society is not only another aspect of the depression, but may indeed be a contributory cause of it. It is significant to note that "Anglo conformity" has been the most "prevalent ideology of assimilation goals in America." It is based on the dominance of English institutions, language, and cultural patterns, which become the standard of what is American.[27] It is also based on the superiority of the Anglo-Saxon culture as the source of greatness of America and the fear that the mixing with "foreign" cultural strains might indeed contaminate it.[28] The national character is conceived to be formed and fixed, and immigrants are to be assimilated within it. It demands a complete renunciation of the immigrant's culture in favor of the behavior and values of the Anglo-Saxon. It found expression in the many nativist movements in our nation's

27. Gordon, pp. 96–97. See E. Digby Baltzell, *The Protestant Establishment* (New York: Random House, 1964).

28. John Hingham, *Strangers in the Land* (New York: Atheneum, 1963), pp. 158–234.

past, from the Know Nothings to the Americanization movement of the 1920s.[29] Its long history need not detain us here.
Suffice it to say that with the new immigration a more
hysterical and often violent expression of this notion was
clearly evident. As Gordon notes,

> Previously vague and romantic notions of Anglo Saxon people-
> hood were combined with general ethnocentrism, rudimentary
> wisps of genetics, selected tidbits of evolutionary theory, and
> naive assumptions from early and crude imported anthropology
> . . . to produce the doctrine that the English, Germans, and
> others of the "old immigration" constituted a superior race . . .
> whereas the peoples of Eastern and Southern Europe made up
> . . . the inferior breeds whose presence in America threatened,
> either by intermixture or supplementation, the traditional
> American stock and culture.[30]

Large-scale Italian immigration was treated by many as "the
Italian problem."[31] The question was variously phrased but,
narrowed down to its roots, it became: What to do with the
Italian? The reaction to the new immigrant hordes in general and the Italian in particular took many forms. There
was outright discrimination, appeals for restricting immigration, and assaults both verbal and physical.[32] The muck-
raking press particularly inveighed against the Italian, seiz-
ing upon what it decided was the inherent criminality of
Italians.[33] At various times these outbursts reached hysterical
proportions.

If there is anything in America that might be held up
as an overall American culture serving as a referent for
the immigrant, it can best be described as, "the middle class
cultural patterns of largely, white Protestant, Anglo-Saxon

---

29. *Ibid.*
30. Gordon, p. 97.
31. Broughton Brandenburg, *Imported Americans* (New York: Fred Stokes
Publishers, 1904) .
32. Hingham.
33. Salvatore Mondello, *"The Italian Immigrant in America 1880–1920."*
(Ph.D. dissertation, New York University, 1960) .

origins."[34] Most of the members of the control group interviewed either reacted negatively or were at least cool to the idea of an ethnic handing on either the language or the cultural heritage of the country of origin to his children. Most thought being "American" was a conscious choice on the part of the immigrant. The choice was the renunciation of all prior identification for that of being "an American." Most tended to view America as groups of unassimilated ethnics and seemed to be uneasy with either appeals to or expressions of ethnic pride.[35]

Historically, there is no evidence to indicate that white Protestant America ever firmly welcomed the new immigrants.[36] On the other hand, it should be noted that the new immigrants did not want immediate structural assimilation since they desired the security of their own institutions.[37] Despite its public expressions of welcome and acceptance, the core society never intended to open up its primary group life to the new immigrant. Gordon asserts,

> The second generation thought they were welcomed to the social cliques, clubs and institutions of the white Protestant America. After all, it was simply a matter of learning American ways . . . and were they not culturally different from their parents the greenhorns?[38]

But they found that at the primary group level a neutral American group structure was a myth.

---

34. Gordon, p. 72. Gordon refers to this group as the core subsociety and the cultural patterns of this group as the core subculture.

35. Charles Price, "Southern Europeans in Australia: The Problem of Assimilation," *IMR* (Summer 1968), pp. 3–26, Richardson notes that the same demands based on Anglo conformity were made upon the southern European immigrants in Australia.

36. *Ibid.* See Mondello, "The Italian Immigrant in America 1880–1920"; John Mariano, *The Italian Contribution to American Democracy* (Boston: Christopher Publishing House, 1921); William Foote Whyte, "Race Conflicts in the North End of Boston," *New England Quarterly* (December 1939); Donald Simmons, "Anti-Italian-American Riddles in New England," *Journal of American Folklore* (February 1966), pp. 475–78.

37. Gordon, p. 72. See also Fitzpatrick, pp. 5–16.

38. *Ibid.*, pp. 111–12.

What at a distance seemed to be a quasi-public edifice flying
only the all-inclusive flag of American nationality turned out
. . . to be the clubhouse of a particular ethnic group—the white
Anglo-Saxon Protestants, its operation shot through with the
promises and expectations of its parental ethnicity . . . [but
it turned out to be] acculturation without massive structural
intermingling at primary group levels has been the dominant
motif in the American experience.[39]

Marcello in almost sorrowful tones lamented, "I thought
Americans were friendly and that I would get into society
right away. This did not happen. I found it very hard.
Society is different here, the customs and laws prevent you
from advancing. I did not like the menial work I had to
take."[40] Gaetano sensed the same thing, "I had always heard
that there were opportunities here you couldn't get elsewhere. I now have a different impression."[41] Most of the
Italian immigrants interviewed felt that being Italian was
perceived as a hindrance to advancement in American society. The most recent arrivals still in the "elation" stage
tended not to see their nationality as a hindrance to their
advancement.[42] Rafaello was typical of them, asserting,
"Italians show that after they struggle they will work their
way up . . . they will show they are as good as any other
group." Those who felt similarly, however, admitted in
other portions of the interview that discrimination against
Italians existed. All fifteen of the immigrants interviewed
felt that the image of Italians held by Americans was a low
one.[43] Some, like Rafaello, explained it in terms of just a

39. *Ibid.*, pp. 113–14. See also Peter Schragg, *Decline of the Wasp* (New
York: Simon and Schuster, 1970) ; Oscar Handlin, *Race and Nationality in
American Life* (New York: Doubleday & Co., Inc., 1957) ; Michael Novak,
The Rise of the Unmeltable Ethnics (New York: Macmillan Co., 1972) .
    40. Interview, Marcello (insurance salesman) .
    41. Interview, Gaetano (dye house worker) .
    42. Question #50. Do you think it helps a person to get ahead to be an
Italian? (Italian-American)
    43. Question #51. How do you think people generally in this country
feel about Italians? Do you think there's much prejudice against them?
        a. What do you think is responsible for it?
        b. Are there any particular groups prejudiced against Italians?

general attitude of impatience with foreigners. Most, like Mina, attributed it to American inability to see and appreciate "differences in groups, their customs and heritage."[44] Many of her fellow immigrants like Donato attributed it to the association of Italians with crime. Donato bellowed angrily, "We are not thought of very highly . . . our overall image is one of crime . . . the Mafia. This is unfair."[45] There was little variation in the responses between the immigrants and the first-generation respondents. All five of the latter agreed that being Italian did not help them to get ahead. As Bob warned, "Once you're outside your neighborhood you're in for rough going."[46]

There is no difference among the generational groupings with regard to the image of Italians held by the rest of society. To Paul, a first-generation respondent, it was definitely a case of discrimination, not only against Italians but against all minorities. "A few do spoil the image . . . but the inability to speak the language, lack of skills and poor education, which was not their fault, led to prejudice, and stereotypes."[47] Mario asserted firmly, "There is most definitely prejudice and discrimination in American corporations. I've seen men with Irish names or WASPs with no greater background or ability move up. Working harder did not help. If one looks at the higher echelons of the corporation you will see a predominance of WASPs or Irish."[48] There is little variation between these sentiments and those of the second generation respondents.

All five of the second generation felt that their nationality was a barrier to advancement. They also agreed with the first-generation respondents that the image of Italians held by Americans was low. The same factors are cited as

44. Interview, Mina (student).
45. Interview, Donato (pattern designer).
46. Interview, Bob (printer).
47. Interview, Paul (college student).
48. Interview, Mario (lawyer). See Baltzell, pp. 315–34.

in the stereotype of Italians as criminals. Lou, a second-generation respondent, sounded like Mario when he asserted that, "If you are of English background it will definitely help you get ahead."[49] Sal declared, "If your name ends in a vowel, your name immediately conjures an association with the Mafia. Even if you're capable, you're not given a better job if you're Italian."[50]

While all the third-generation respondents agreed that the image of Italians was low, they did not feel that it was great enough to hinder them from advancement. The reasons given by the third generation for this state of affairs varied. Father Andrew felt that the Italian is stereotyped. "This made the Italian defensive. The banding together was necessary before. The way to deal with it is not being defensive but to be sure of yourself and do things which are right and good. You can do good without being Italian."[51] Laura attributed the low image to a stereotype of Italians as being "non-intellectually oriented . . . being workers not thinkers."[52] Carmen saw it as a stereotype of the Italians' physical features: ". . . they [Americans] think of them as lower class."[53] Sal, a second-generation respondent, sounded like a number of others when he contended that "a lot of Irish and WASPs are at the head of things . . . these major groups don't let other people get ahead."[54]

Nearly all the immigrant respondents had encountered some form of prejudice, while most of the first- and second-generation respondents had similar experiences.[55] Fewer of the third-generation respondents said that they encountered any prejudice. Nearly all of the respondents felt that T.V.

49. Interview, Lou (clock checker) .
50. Interview, Sal (undertaker) .
51. Interview, Father Andrew (priest) .
52. Interview, Laura (student) .
53. Interview, Carmen (college student) .
54. Interview, Sal.
55. Question #52. Have you ever felt discriminated against because of your nationality?

shows giving unsavory characters Italian names was a form
of prejudice.[56] Most of the Italian immigrants interviewed,
when asked if most big gangsters were Italian, felt with
Donato that "there are many nationalities involved in
crime.[57] One has to remember that there are many forms
of crime which involves politicians, businessmen, the con-
sumer market, and so forth. There are different forms of
crime. There are different nationalities in organized crime.
I know it. I see it in my own field. If you just go according
to the papers, an immediate link with the Mafia is made
with any Italian who commits a crime or is even suspected
. . . [whereas] anyone else doing exactly the same thing
goes without making such a link."[58] Significantly, the first-
and second-generation respondents on the whole agreed,
while those of the third generation, on the contrary, felt
that most big gangsters were Italian.

If the Italian immigrant feels more satisfied than dissatisfied, then the basis is established for the development of a
sense of attachment and belonging to American society.[59]
When this occurs, he has reached the identification level of
assimilation, which Gordon has defined as the "development of the sense of peoplehood based exclusively on the
host society."[60] Being identified with the host group implies
a favorable set of attitudes that can result in the adoption
of a wider range of beliefs, attitudes, and values. Satisfaction, however, has no implications for any change in the

---

56. Question #53. Some people have complained that T.V., radio, etc. are
giving their gangster characters Italian names. Have you been aware of
this? Would you consider this a form of prejudice? See Giulio Miranda,
"From the Italo Think Tank" *Italo-American Times* (September 1972),
p. 8.; Francis A. J. Ianni, *A Family Business* (New York: Russell Sage
Foundation, 1972); Luciano Iorizzio, ed., *An Inquiry Into Organized Crime*
(Staten Island, N. Y.: American-Italian Historical Association, 1970).

57. Question #54. Do you think there is any truth to the view that most
big gangsters and racketeers in this country are of Italian descent? Why?

58. Interview, Donato.

59. Richardson, pp. 6–12.

60. Gordon, pp. 71–83.

Italian's feelings of group identity.[61] It is the base upon which a changed identity may be constructed.

A change in group identity rarely goes to the point of an outright exchange of group identities.[62] This is borne out by our respondents who gave no evidence of a complete exchange of identities. All but five of the immigrants interviewed thought of themselves as Italian, the others identified as Italian-American. All of the first- and second-generation respondents identified as Italian-Americans, as well as most of those of the third generation. The immigrant respondents also felt that non-Italians viewed them as Italian, so that identification and outside perception were in conformity to one another.[63] The first- and second-generation respondents who identified as Italian-American were perceived by others as being Italian. To most of them, an Italian-American identification was not incompatible with being "American" and, therefore, the perception of others as being Italian seemed to connote an exclusion. Sal, an undertaker and the oldest respondent interviewed, recounted his experience. "Always among Americans I was 'the' Italian. It was used in the sense that I was an outsider. To them, and used in this sense, I will always be an outsider. This became a stigma and I therefore became 'the' Italian undertaker. My business became restricted to only Italians, not by their doing or efforts but by the stigma of the general community. This resulted in a greatly restricted business."[64]

---

61. Jerold Heiss, "Sources of Satisfaction and Assimilation Among Immigrants," *Human Relations* (May 1966), pp. 165–77. See also Glaser, "Dynamics of Ethnic Identification," *ASR* (*February* 1958), pp. 31–40; Tamatsu Shibutani and Kiav Kwan, *Ethnic Stratification* (New York: Macmillan Co., 1965), pp. 27–55, 199–223.

62. V. C. Nahirny and J. A. Fishman, "American Immigrant Group: Ethnic Identification and the Problem of Generations," *Sociological Review* (November 1965).

63. Question #54. How do you think of yourself, as an Italian, Italian-American or American?
    a. How do you feel other people think of you?

64. Interview, Sal.

Laura, a third-generation student, felt similarly. "I'm going out with an Irish boy. When I'm introduced to his friends or relatives it's as 'the Italian,' almost as if it seems to have a bearing on my character. Most others see me in the same light . . . as an Italian."[65] With one exception, identification and perception among third-generation respondents were in agreement.

All of the immigrant respondents asserted their sense of closeness with Italian ways as opposed to American ways of life.[66] All of the first-, second-, and third-generation respondents felt closer to American ways of life. Paul is typical of those of the first generation in this regard when he declared proudly, "Most of my life has been spent here . . . so I feel closer to American ways. I've adopted the culture and in turn I have forgotten many of the Italian customs."[67]

The above findings reaffirm our contention that an Italian-American identification is not viewed by the respondents as being incompatible with being American, since they do feel closer to the American way of life. However, conflict does develop when the individual senses that the broader society does make the distinction by holding that the two are incompatible. This produces some self-doubt, as in the case of Larry, a first-generation automotive repair dealer. "I feel closer to the American way of life but it's an Italianized version of what American life is like. I am closer to Anglo-Saxon ideas as far as business is concerned. I don't know the real American way of life, but only the Italian idea of it."[68]

There is some reaction to this "supposed" incompatibility when the pressures from the host society reach the point of

---

65. Interview, Laura.
66. Question #46. Do you feel closer to the Italian or American way of life? Why? Which has influenced you the most?
67. Interview, Paul.
68. Interview, Larry (auto dealer).

changing identification by name alteration.[69] All of the immigrants, and first- and second-generation respondents interviewed resented Italians changing their name under any circumstance. The third-generation respondents felt the same way, but tended to condition their disapproval with the situation. For Rafaéllo the persistence of being Italian was the overriding factor. "This is a great mistake. You don't change your blood. You'll always be Italian."[70] Many of the second-generation respondents, like Larry, look to personality defects to explain it. "I'm sorry for them, since they are trying to escape from reality," he said.[71] Sal on the other hand declared, "I have no use for people who change their names. I can only think they have something to hide or are afraid of something."[72] Laura, a third-generation respondent, felt similarly: ". . . just to hide being Italian for the sake of being American by renouncing yourself is actually denying yourself. It's sad."[73] Vincent was a little more understanding, but equally adamant: "I can understand if it's necessary to get work . . . that is, for survival. I'm ashamed of anyone doing it. I would hope this kind of pressure will end."[74] Another index of identification is the kind of group with which the respondents identify or feel close. Nearly all of the immigrant respondents preferred Italians from Italy, while all of the first-, second-, and most of the third-generation respondents felt closer to Italian-Americans.[75]

The immigrant and first- and second-generation respon-

---

69. Question #58. Have you ever thought of changing your name so that it would not be taken for being Italian? What is your opinion of such changes?

70. Interview, Rafaello (restaurant worker).

71. Interview, Larry.

72. Interview, Sal.

73. Interview, Laura.

74. Interview, Vincent (college student).

75. Question #49. Which of these groups do you like best or identify with the most?

    a. Italians born and raised in Italy.

    b. Americans of Italian descent.

    c. Americans of non-Italian descent.

dents considered their parents for the most part Italianized, while those of the third generation considered theirs Americanized.[76]

Still another index of identification is the relative constancy of interest in things Italian. Only three of the immigrants felt that their interest in Italian things had actually declined; for most it either remained constant or had increased. Significantly, all first-, second-, and most third-generation respondents indicated that their interest in Italian things had increased from their early years.[77]

The Italian immigrant is less likely to attain rapid identificational assimilation if he has strong family ties or obligations to someone in Italy. If these factors are absent from the immigrant situation, and he lacks economic or emotional resources, he is more apt to become dependent on his adopted country. He will in turn be more sensitive to expressions of approval and disapproval emerging from the host society. Most of the immigrants interviewed keep in fairly regular contact with members of their family in Italy either by letter or by mailing packages.[78] This kind of contact declines in the first generation and drops off sharply in the second and third generation. All of the immigrants interviewed felt homesick for Italy at some time or another, but in varying intensity and frequency.[79] Most of the immigrants said they would like to return to visit Italy and would feel good doing so.[80] But there was a division of opinion as to how they would actually feel. Half expressed views that they would feel happy. As Mina described her return visit,

---

76. Question #48. Would you consider your parents Italianized or Americanized?

77. Question #47. As you have grown older, have you become more or less interested in Italian things?

78. Question #71. Do you write regularly to friends or relatives in Italy? How often?
    a. Do you send money or packages to them?

79. Question #68. Are you ever homesick for Italy?

80. Question #67. How do you think you would feel if you went back to Italy? Have you ever returned? Do you intend to return? Why would you return?

"When I returned I felt freer there than here. I should never have gone back, because I was greatly attracted to the life I had left."[81] The other half, like Donato, said that it would necessitate a readjustment. "The first week I was here I wanted to go back right away. . . . I did return not long ago, but I realized it would be difficult to adjust to Italian ways of life."[82] The Italian immigrant who knows that he has the emotional and economic means to reemigrate is less likely to be identified with being American.

When major changes in attitudes, beliefs, and behaviors have occurred, then the acculturation level of assimilation has been reached. Gordon refers to this as cultural assimilation, or the adoption of those basic values and patterns of behavior of the host culture which enable the newcomers to function effectively in the host society.[83] All but four of the immigrant respondents said in varying frequency that they tended to translate American dollars mentally into Italian liras.[84] This tendency, however, weakens rapidly, and the absence of its persistence correlates positively with the length of residence of the respondent. None of the members of the first generation interviewed gave any evidence of going through this mental association. While there were varying rates of frequency, all but two of the immigrants did follow a sport or activity associated with Italy.[85] There is a similar rate of persistence in the first generation, but a significant and sharp drop into the second and third. The most frequent sport mentioned by the immigrants and first-generation respondents is soccer, while the assumption of

81. Interview, Mina.
82. Interview, Donato.
83. Gordon, p. 71. See also Melford Spiro, "The Acculturation of American Ethnic Groups," *American Anthropologist* (December 1955), pp. 1240–51.
84. Question #72. When someone tells you a price in U. S. dollars do you ever translate it mentally to Italian liras?
85. Question #78. Do you follow any sports or events associated with Italy, e.g., soccer, opera? See also Francis Ianni, "Time and Place as Variables in Acculturation Research," *American Anthropologist* (February 1958), pp. 39–45.

American values is seen in the association with football or baseball by those of the second and third generation. Nearly all of the immigrants found themselves rooting for an Italian, either in sports, politics, or some other activity.[86] While this pattern continues into the second generation, there is some ambiguity, some hesitation, in making a choice indicating a change of values and patterns of behavior. The second generation gave greater evidence of crossing ethnic lines in a similar situation, even though there was a strong attachment to the Italian. Most of the third-generation respondents rarely choose on strictly ethnic lines to root for the Italian participant in the activity. When given an absolute situation of an American facing an Italian team, there was mixed opinion on the part of the immigrants, some hesitation, but then a final selection of the American side by the first generation, but a firm choice of the American team by both the second- and third-generation respondents. The preference for Italian food is a particularly important source of identification among Italians.[87] There is a strong preference for Italian food over American among the immigrants and first-generation respondents, with some evidence of mixture of food patterns among those of the second, and a definite mixture weighted on the side of American patterns among those of the third generation. By the second generation, there is little evidence of the variety of Italian cuisine, or of the more traditional aspects of it that are more clearly evident during holidays.[88]

We may also look at another dimension of the acculturation of Italians, the changes in its occupational and residential structure that tell us not only of their changing status, but their acculturation. If we were to find Italians in higher-status positions, it would indicate not only the ac-

86. Question #79. Did you ever find yourself rooting for the Italian in sports or politics or something like that?

87. Question #73. Which do you prefer to eat most of the time, American or Italian style food?

88. Gans, pp. 34-35.

ceptance by the host society, but the acquisition of the necessary skills to occupy these positions. When we survey the
occupational categories of all three groups, the major classification that they fall into is semi-skilled or skilled occupations.[89] Only three of the respondents fall into the professional category, one being a lawyer, the other two priests.[90]
When we consider income level, only one second-, and one
third-generation respondent could be considered in an upper
income category of $20,000 to $24,999. Most of the immigrants and third-generation respondents were in the lower
income bracket of $4,000 to $7,999. Most of the first- and
second-generation respondents tended to be in the moderate
income bracket from $8,000 to $15,999.[91]

The out-migration of Italians into the better residential
areas would indicate the further acceptance of the host society, and the willingness to break with the ethnic enclave.[92]
The movement of Italians from the lower to the higher
levels of the residential and occupational hierarchies is not
only an index of social mobility of Italians, but a sign that
a positive relationship is established between upward mobility and acculturation. I have dealt substantially with residence patterns in an earlier chapter. Suffice it to say here
that the persistence of residential segregation, the persistence
and stability of Italian neighborhoods, does not provide
evidence of the acceptance of Italians by the host society.[93]

89. Francis Ianni, "Residential and Occupational Mobility as Indices of
the Acculturation of an Ethnic Group," Social Forces (October 1957).
90. Price, p. 9. Price provides interesting contrasts for the researcher regarding occupational assimilation.
91. Lieberson, "The Impact of Residential Segregation on Ethnic Assimilation," Social Forces (October 1961), p. 56. The occupational composition of highly segregated ethnic groups will tend to be more sharply differentiated from that of native whites. Lieberson constructs an index of such
differentiation of Italians from the native white population in five American
cities.
92. Coming to feel more like a typical member of the host society is not
the same as coming to be more like one. Identification involves a subjective
feeling, while acculturation, when it occurs, is an objective state of affairs.
93. Duncan and Lieberson, p. 364. See also Jerold Heiss, "Residential Segregation and Assimilation of Italians in an Australian City," IMR (Spring,
1966), pp. 165–71.

The new residences in effect become Italian-American neighborhoods.

Evidence of a mixture in the ethnic composition of the neighborhoods of the second- and the third-generation respondents indicates that acculturation has taken place. My findings regarding the occupational patterns of Italians lead to the same conclusion. When we consider the acculturation in all its dimensions, we find that the Italian becomes acculturated at a rapid pace, and the process is complete to a large extent in the first generation.[94] However, the occupational data and the residential patterns discussed earlier support the conclusion that structural assimilation has not taken place among the Italians studied.

When I looked at marriage patterns among the three-generation sample, I found that all of the respondents have parents who were Italian.[95] Of those who were married, all chose Italian mates. Most of the Italian immigrants interviewed were not inclined to marry non-Italians; however, the first-generation respondents were even more resistant to the idea than the immigrant group. Despite some equivocation, most of the first-generation respondents inclined toward Italian mates. Paul, for example, asserted, "I don't have a preference . . . but I'm more likely to marry an Italian girl because of our mutual background and understanding."[96] Bob, on the other hand, assured me, "I thought a lot about it . . . but my view changes. I know one thing —I wouldn't want my children to be completely cut off from the Italian heritage."[97] Among the second-generation Italian-Americans, most were like Lou, who said, "I mar-

---

94. Gans, pp. 34–35.
95. The proportion of those having a mixed parentage would seem to be inversely related to magnitude of the Italian immigrants' segregation from the native white population (see chapter 1). The more segregated the Italian population, the more likely a greater proportion of in-group marriages.
96. Interview, Paul.
97. Interview, Bob.

ried an Italian girl. As far as my sons are concerned, I'll go along with whatever makes them happy. If they ask me I'll tell them that living with someone like yourself makes it easier to get along . . . but, it would be their choice."[98]

Among third-generation respondents there was a strong tendency to be more receptive to marrying a non-Italian. Thus, a predilection for out-group marriages is present in the second and third generations, but my findings are inconclusive on this point.

B. R. Bugleski found that the 1930 pattern of in-group marriages had been reversed in 1960, when two thirds of the marriages studied involved partners from different ethnic groups.[99] He also found that Italians in Buffalo had a higher rate of out-group marriages than any other group studied, and asserts confidently that by 1975 the Italian wedding will be a thing of the past.

Kennedy, in her study of intermarriage rates from 1870 to 1950 in New Haven, found an increasing trend toward the breaking-down of national-origins barriers in marriage. However, she found a "triple melting pot" effect in which interethnic marriages tended to take place within the three major religions: Catholic, Protestant, and Jewish. While de-declining, the in-marriage rates for certain ethnic groups were still high. While the rate for Italians had fallen in New Haven from 97.1% in 1900, it declined to only 76.70 in 1950. Thus, as late as 1950, 75% of Italians in New Haven selected mates who were also Italian.[100]

While our findings can neither support or refute the above in absolute terms there is some inferential support. However, we do suggest that the more segregated the Italians, the more there was the tendency for in-group mar-

---

98. Interview, Lou.
99. B. R. Bugleski, "Assimilation Through Intermarriage," *Social Forces* (December 1961), p. 147.
100. Ruby Jo Reeves Kennedy, "Single or Triple Melting Pot? Intermarriage Trends in New Haven, 1870–1940," *AJS* (January 1944), p. 56.

riages; and the more recently arrived the more segregated.[101]

Another dimension to the acculturation of Italians is along religious lines. While this study was not constructed to deal with this aspect of acculturation, I can report on the findings of Professor Russo. Russo hypothesized that in religious matters, increased Americanization would bring about an increasing resemblance to Irish norms. Italians reacted to Irish Catholicism in three ways. First, by conforming, and second, by internalizing Irish-American religious norms. Finally, they challenged those norms, either from within or from without the Catholic Church. Most followed the first two courses of action. The Catholic Church and its school system have contributed to the cultural assimilation of Italians in New York City. The intermingling of the Italian-American in the Irish Church and parochial schools fostered out-group marriages. Russo, to prove his point regarding the conformity to Irish norms, examines church attendance, reception of Holy Communion, family size, and parochial school education across a three-generational span, and then compares it with the Irish. He concludes that while there is some retention of identity, there is an absorption of the cultural patterns of American-Irish society. In addition, social assimilation into the primary Catholic groups is well underway.[102]

Conclusion

The principal variables that determine the process of the Italian immigrant's assimilation are his basic motivations

---

101. In a larger sample, I would suspect that the proportion of second- and third-generation people having mixed parentage would be inversely related to the extent they are segregated from the native white population. See Nicholas John Russo, "Three Generations of Italians in New York City: Their Religious Acculturation," *IMR* 3 (Spring 1969). Russo supports Bugleski's findings in concluding that there was an increasing number of out-group marriages across a three-generational span.

102. *Ibid.* See also Glazer and Moynihan, pp. 202–5.

and role expectations, and the demands made upon him in the United States. Italian immigrants are frustrated with aspects of Italian society and were unable to achieve or fulfill their aspirations. The immigrant develops certain expectations about his future role in American society. The Italian immigrant feels that certain instrumental goals, especially economic ones, will be attained in America. Upon leaving Italy, the immigrant detaches himself from any of the roles he had performed. As a result of a number of factors as family-link immigration, out-group rejection, and the need for security and satisfaction, his life is centered in the Italian enclave, which restricts his participation to only a few roles. His lack of work skills and language limits his assumption of new roles and marks him off from the rest of society. Gradually he finds it necessary to rebuild and reform his ideas of himself by acquiring a new set of values and testing them out in relation to the new roles. The Italian possesses a low self-image, one that conforms to the one held of Italian immigrants by the broader society.

The institutionalization of the Italian's behavior occurs within the social structure of the United States. An out-group rejection is conveyed in the demands and expectations made of him and in his limitation to certain roles. The Italian perceives the social and political process to be dominated by members of the core society.

While the Italian acculturates rapidly, there is no outright exchange of group identities. The Italian immigrant identifies as an Italian while the first-, second-, and third-generation respondents identified as Italian-Americans. On the whole, the Italian still favors in-group marriages, although there is evidence of a predilection to marry non-Italians by the second and third generation.

The Italian has acculturated rapidly and the process is usually complete by the first generation. He is assimilated only in part on the other levels: attitude receptional, be-

havior receptional, marital, and civic. However, total identificational assimilation has not taken place.[103]

The most important level of assimilation finds the Italian structurally unassimilated, as evidenced by an occupational and residential differentiation from the core society.[104] Few of the respondents in all groups could be listed
in the higher income, better residential, and upper occupational categories.

A structural separation of the Italian results in the retention and solidification of an Italian identiy. It also causes
the Italian subsociety to persist.

103. I have previously defined this as the sense of identity based entirely
on the host society.

104. Harry C. Dillingham, "Protestant Religion and Social Status," *AJS*
(January 1965), pp. 416–22.

4

Ethnicity, Religion, and Class

I discussed earlier the interaction of certain stimuli and predispositions in the creation of the Italian subsociety. I also noted the relationship of structural assimilation to the creation of the subsociety. The intent of this chapter is to explore the same kind of interaction by considering the roles of ethnicity, religion, and class in the Italian's perception of political life.

I might refer to the Italian subsociety that is created by the intersection of the vertical stratifications of ethnicity and the horizontal stratifications of social class, such as "the ethniclass." A specific ethniclass serves as a reference group in the minds of other Italians. The tangible units of the subsociety are localized in space in particular communities. The Italian subcommunities are linked with each other by class and Italian-typed institutions, friendships, and organizations across communities to form the Italian subsociety. An Italian cultural and social identity can persist with the loss of an ecological base.

The retention of a cultural and social identity results in

making ethniclass membership an important stimulus influencing the perceptions held by Italian-Americans; moreover, it becomes part of their perceptual screen.

A lack of structural assimilation is reflected in Italian-Americans' absence as a group in the higher occupational, income, and residential categories. The persistence of an Italian-American subsociety makes group advancement important to it; hence, it causes members of the subsociety to be responsive to the politics of recognition. Religion and ethnicity become major determinants of the ideological orientation of Italian-Americans on a local level.[1]

At the outset I might attempt to clarify ethniclass. An Italian-American's ethniclass might be lower-middle-class, white, Italian-Catholic, while someone else might be lower-upper-class, white, Anglo-Saxon Protestant. Differences of social class may be more important and decisive than differences of ethnic group. People of the same social class tend to act alike and to have the same values even if they have a different ethnic background. The greatest resemblance is among people of the same social-class segment within the same ethnic group; i.e., the ethniclass.

The sense that one is bound up with "his people" might be called historical identification. In this sense the ethnic group is the locus of historical identification.[2] A sense of comfort with certain people, leading to frequent participation with them and shared behavioral similarities, might be called participational identification. With a person of the same social class but of a different ethnic group,[3] one shares behavioral similarities but not a sense of peoplehood.[4] With

1. I will discuss the impact of social class on party preference on the national level in chapter 7.

2. The use of this concept as the basis for this discussion is drawn entirely from Milton Gordon, *Assimilation in American Life* (New York: Oxford University Press, 1964), p. 51.

3. Ethnicity might be called a sense of peoplehood. A group with a shared feeling of peoplehood is an ethnic group. *Ibid.*, p. 24. See also Oscar Handlin, *Race and Nationality in American Life* (Boston: Little Brown, 1957).

4. Gordon, p. 53. See also M. Plax, "On Studying Ethnicity," *POQ* (Spring 1972), pp. 99–104.

those of the same ethnic group but of a different social class, one shares the sense of peoplehood but not behavioral similarities. The only group that meets both of these criteria are people of the same ethnic group and same social class. American society may be conceived as a mosaic of ethnic groups based on race, religion, and national origin, interlaced by social-class stratification to form the characteristic subsocietal unit, the ethniclass.

Each subsociety, such as lower-middle-class Italians, exists as a reference group in the minds of other Italians. The tangible units of each subsociety are localized in space in particular communities. Thus, one might speak of the lower-middle-class Italians of Paterson or the upper-class, white, Anglo-Saxon Protestants of Boston. These subcommittees in the various communities are connected with each other, in part by class and ethnic-typed institutions and organizations that are national in scope, and in part by class and ethnic-typed friendships across community lines. They are more importantly connected by the ability of each person in a given ethniclass to move to another community and take his place within the same segment of the population marked off by ethnic group and social class. The sum of these subcommunities, interwoven by the various national institutions and organizations that are characteristic of that particular ethnic group and social class, constitutes the Italian-American subsociety.[5] As Etzioni observes, "A group can maintain its cultural and social integration and identity, without having an ecological basis." The subcommunity is not necessarily a geographical location but rather a social construct in the minds of its residents.[6]

In earlier pages I made a distinction between cultural and structural assimilation. The conclusion was that the structural separation of Italians in particular, and ethnic groups

5. Gordon, pp. 160–63.
6. Amitai Etzioni, "The Ghetto—a Re-Evaluation," *Social Forces* (March 1959), pp. 255–62.

in general, has been brought about by the historic position that the core society has taken toward the members of minority groups.[7] Cultural assimilation has proceeded rapidly among the Italians, and is complete to a large extent by the second generation. The institutionalization of the Italian's behavior takes place within the American social structure, and that structure serves to exclude him from certain roles and limits him to others.[8]

In view of these findings, what role does ethnicity play in the Italian's perceptions of political life and his political behavior? While Italians shed many of their cultural traits rapidly, the persistence of some identification, however weak or intense, is clearly evident among all of the groups interviewed. For example, all of the respondents were conscious of an Italian name when reading a newspaper or in everyday life.[9] Most of the respondents in all groups tended to gauge the nationalities of people when they came across names in everyday life.[10] Name identification and its retention by all the respondents is an important link with their Italian past. Another strong link with the Italian past about which I reported earlier is the preference for Italian food across the three-generational span.

In terms of political advancement, all expressed an interest in seeing "their own kind" get ahead in political life.[11] Most of the respondents thought that most Italians were

---

7. See chapter 3.

8. I will discuss the political implications of a lack of structural assimilation in chapters 5, 6, and 7. See Richard Krickus, "The White Ethnic: Who Are they And Where Are They going?", *City Magazine* (June 1971) , and Michael Novak, *The Rise of the Unmeltable Ethnics* (New York: Macmillan Co., 1972) .

9. Question #60. When you come across an Italian name in the newspaper or in everyday life are you aware that the name is Italian?

10. Question #61. Do you often try to gauge the nationalities of people? Question #62. Do you think it sometimes helps to understand other people if you know their national origins?

11. Question #82. Are you interested in seeing Italians get ahead in politics?

Democrats.[12] The Italians from all groups tended to prefer the Italian candidate rather than the non-Italian, regardless of party. When the party was removed and the respondents were placed in an absolute situation in which the alternatives between the Italian and non-Italian candidates was premised on their being of equal ability, they all chose the Italian candidate.[13]

The reason for the persistence of ethnicity as a factor in the Italians perceptions of political life is based on an earlier conclusion.[14] The Italian has not been structurally assimilated into the core society. We have seen the attempts by Italians to reestablish their former communities in America. While they were largely successful in doing just this, they were unable to transplant their way of life exactly and in every detail. Furthermore, it would be an exaggeration to say it persisted in a vacuum outside the reach of the larger society. Their native ways had to undergo some change. The Italian language underwent a change and what emerged was an Italo-American dialect.[15] By the first generation, and definitely by the second generation, acculturation is complete, and interest in the Italian culture has dropped sharply.[16] Despite cultural assimilation, the Italians have

---

12. Question #83. Do you feel most Italians are Democrats or Republicans?
   a. If Democrats—Suppose the Italians were running on the Republican ticket and the non-Italians on the Democratic ticket, which would you vote for?
   b. Reverse the situation if they choose Republican.

13. Question #81. If you had to choose between two men of equal ability or had no political difference, and one was of Italian descent and the other non-Italian . . . for whom would you vote?

14. Raymond Wolfinger, "The Development and Persistence of Ethnic Voting Group," *American Politcal Science Review* (December 1965). Wolfinger presents a number of alternate explanations; however, they lack substantiating data and do not answer the hard question posed at the outset of this chapter.

15. Words like cake became caka; street—stritto; car—carro; store—storo. See Josephine Butera, "A Study of the Italo-American Dialect; Adaptation Into the Italian Language or Dialects for the Purpose of Adjustment in an Italo-American Environment" (M.A. thesis) , (New York University, 1941) .

16. Oscar Handlin, *Boston's Immigrants, A Study in Acculturation* (Cambridge: Harvard University Press, 1959) ; W. L. Warner and Leo Srole, *The*

maintained a social substructure that takes into account both their primary and secondary relations.[17] Hence, the Italians in particular and the ethnic group in general bear a special relationship to the social structure.[18] Both Whyte and Gans have noted that American styles, language, sports, and the like predominated among the Italian-Americans of Boston, but personal relations and social group structures were almost exclusively Italian-American in both the North End in the 1940s and the West End in the 1950s.[19] The same conclusion was reached with the Italians of the New York metropolitan area.[20] As Parenti observes,

> For ethnic social sub-systems may persist or evolve new structures independent of the host society and despite dramatic cultural transitions in the direction of the mainstream culture.[21]

We found earlier that there has been no substantial movement by our respondents into the higher occupational and residential levels. Even if individual Italians may have entered professional and occupational roles beyond the reach of their fathers or, previously, themselves, the group mobility of the Italians has not been substantial.[22] When we look at the occupational positions of the first- and second-generation Italians, there is no substantial convergence of intergenerational status levels. The same holds true of a similar generational comparison of other ethnic groups.[23]

Social Systems of American Ethnic Groups (New Haven: Yale University Press, 1945) . See Herbert Gans, *The Urban Villagers* (New York: The Free Press, 1962) .

17. Earlier I discussed the relationship of ethnic group to the social structure.

18. Social structure is employed here to mean man's crystallized social relationships. See Gordon, p. 31.

19. Gans; Whyte, *Street Corner Society.*

20. See chapters 1 and 2.

21. Parenti, *APSR*, pp. 718–19.

22. Warner and Srole, pp. 102, 285–96; Fred Strodtbeck *et al.,* "Evaluation of Occupation: A Reflection of Jewish and Italian Mobility Differences," *ASA* (October 1957) .

23. U. S. Census of Population, 1960.

Thus, ethnic distinctions continue to persist in the stratification system. Movement upward for the Italian-American is less a matter of group mobility than an overall improved standard of living for all Americans. The availability of more white-collar jobs for Italian-Americans is owing to structural changes in the American economy.

The movement from the central city and that of the ethnic enclave to the suburbs does not appear to have an integrative effect.[24] The individual Italian can live most of his life aside from work in a subsocietal network of schools, family, church, and recreation.[25] Suburbs tend toward the establishment of ethnic clusters.[26] The movement to the suburbs may create a tension between the native resident and the new arrival that may reinforce ethnic identification. This same tension may reinforce ethnic political alignments.[27] There is some foundation for the assertion that those Italians who were most segregated from the core society in the central city are also most residentially concentrated in the suburbs. Thus, suburban residential patterns follow those found in the central city.[28]

Residential segregation is not a necessary condition for the Italians in maintaining a subsocial structure. As we have seen, Italians can maintain a social cohesion and identity without an ecological base.[29] While the Italian neighborhood cannot be transplanted exactly as it existed in the city, its features are adapted to suburban living, but not eliminated. Thus, in-group social patterns reinforce an Italian identification.

24. A. C. Spectorsky, *The Ex-Urbanites* (New York: J. B. Lippincott, 1955).

25. Scott Greer, "Catholic Voters and the Democratic Party," *POQ* 25 (1961) : 624.

26. Robert Wood, *Suburbia, Its People and Their Politics* (Boston: Houghton Mifflin Co., 1958), p. 178.

27. *Ibid.*

28. Stanley Lieberson, "Suburbs and Ethnic Residential Patterns," *AJS* 67 (1962) : 673–81.

29. Etzioni, "The Ghetto—a Re-Evaluation." See also Glaser and Moynihan, pp. 13–16.

While there may changes in the social patterns of the Italians, these do not seem to indicate structural assimilation into the core social structure. Nor does the movement of Italians from the city to the Far West indicate that this structural assimilation is taking place elsewhere. In fact, their acculturation may lead to a more ethnic political awareness.[30]

Parallel social structures have emerged, encouraged by a greater affluence. Movement to the higher residential and occupational hierarchies for individual Italians often provides the resources for the establishment of parallel subsocietal structures, rather than their destruction. For example, Protestant clubs that had been exclusionist have engendered the rise of Catholic ethnic clubs.[31] Marymount College is the Catholic counterpart for upper-class Catholic girls of Sarah Lawrence or Vassar for upper-class Protestant girls. As a counterpart of Yale or Princeton, upper-class Catholic boys might choose Notre Dame University, where they might meet girls at nearby St. Mary's College.[32]

What accounts for the persistence of an Italian identification? Parenti has observed,

> Insofar as the individual internalizes experiences from earlier social positions and sub-cultural matrices, his personality may act as a determinant—or character interpreter—of his present socio-cultural world. . . . Just as social assimilation moves along a different and slower path than that of acculturation, so does identity assimilation, or rather non-assimilation enjoy a pertinacity not wholly responsive to the other two processes.[33]

The early experiences with the Italian culture, the persistence and extension of family attachments, and the Italian name provide constant reminders of one's Italianness.

30. Andrew Rolle, *The Immigrant Upraised* (Norman: University of Oklahoma Press, 1968).

31. John R. Ellis, *American Catholicism* (Chicago: University of Chicago Press, 1956).

32. Gordon, pp. 210–11.

33. Parenti, pp. 722–23.

Though acculturated, an Italian-American identification provides the individual with an identity, which may be gone when he becomes a nonethnic. Such an identity becomes increasingly important when living in an urban environment and in a mass society. Moreover, the acculturated Italian-American may be more acceptable to the core society than the unacculturated.[34] But this acceptance does not mean an incorporation into the primary group relations. Even with acceptance, some kind of stigma may attach to being Italian. The persistence of an Italian-American identification and a parallel substructure is based on an out-group rejection. Thus, the greater the feelings of exclusion among our respondents, the more they will identify as Italian-Americans.

Another factor in the persistence of an Italian-American identification that in turn influences their political behavior is the American political system. That system continues to rely on ethnic strategies. The reason that politicians give consideration to ethnic groupings is that ethnic substructures are highly visible and do exist, and that ethnics respond as ethnics.

To the Italian-American, being a member of an ethnic group produces attitudes that have a bearing on his social and political participation. Among these perceptions is an acute sense of subordinate status, the feeling that society underrates him and his group. This holds true of the Italian as well as other ethnic groups. This is grounded not only in subjective estimates but objective reality.

With acculturation the Italian-American is increasingly outward-looking. He senses that he is part of a beleaguered social group and is sensitive to his group's status. He also becomes eager to advance the Italian-American's interest by all available means. While rejection by the core society leads to the establishment of parallel subsocietal structures, it also leads to a certain uneasiness, which will be resolved

34. Warner and Srole, p. 84.

only by individual or group advancement. It also produces a desire for respectability to be won by political recognition. Ethnic conflict emerges quite obviously, since there cannot be enough recognition or resources to go around for all groups. The question of which groups are to get them leads to ethnic conflict.[35] However, the greater the ethnic conflict in a community, the greater the rates of participation of the conflicting groups.[36]

One view of the mayorality campaign interpreted the ethnic role, particularly that of the Italian-Americans, as part of a "backlash." In order to explore the validity of this view, I sought to ascertain the Italian view of different ethnic groups. Toward Jews we found a universally favorable attitude, with no evidence among the respondents of an anti-Semitic attitude. Alfredo, an immigrant, was typical of all respondents. He said, "They are a smart and united people, yet they did so much coming here from so much persecution from different places in the world. They have contributed a great deal to the U. S. and of all the ethnic groups they help each other and others the most."[37] Toward Blacks, Paul and Mario were typical of the vast majority of the respondents. As Paul put it, "Blacks are much more entitled to be full Americans than any group I know. They have not been given the opportunity to the same level. They have been especially discriminated against because of their color."[38] Mario also declared, "All of their claims and protests are well founded."[39] Joe offered what might appear to be a dissent, a mild one at that, "They need opportunities but at some point they must help themselves." Marcello said, "They are human beings and are like everyone else.

---

35. Edward Banfield and James Q. Wilson, *City Politics* (Cambridge, Mass.: Harvard University Press, 1966), pp. 41–46.
36. *Ibid.* p. 42.
37. Interview, Alfredo.
38. Interview, Paul.
39. Interview, Mario. See A. L. Rosenblum, "Ethnic Prejudice as Related to Social Clan and Religiosity," *Sociology and Social Research* (March 1959), pp. 272–75.

Sometimes they overdo protests; there are limits of a protest."[40] The respondents were also favorable toward other ethnic groups. There were a few negative responses toward Puerto Ricans, mainly among a few of the immigrant respondents such as Donato, who claimed, "the majority came to the United States for welfare but there are good and bad."[41] However, the majority of the respondents were well disposed toward them. As Umberto put it, "there are many Puerto Ricans in this area . . . we get along. There are many on my block. They are like all other people. They want the same things we do."[42] Thus, the evidence does not indicate any significant hostility to any ethnic group. There was an especially high tolerance of groups along religious lines.

The more that the Italian becomes conscious of his ethnic identity and his place in society, the more he will be sensitive to the politics of recognition.[43] The locus of Italians' political interests is most often on the local level.[44] This may be because of the historic role of community and region in the Italian past, which persists among succeeding generations of Italians in America. American cities, on the other hand, have not developed an impartial nonpolitical bureaucracy and local magistracy. This results in a mutual reliance between public officials and voter. Rewards are distributed in relation to the voting strength of various groups, ethnic included.[45] During the New York mayoralty campaign, John Lindsay sought to capture the loyalty of the voters of Queens by pressing physical and service improvements for the residents. The area, heavily Italo-American, had severely criticized the mayor for his apparent mishandling of a snow

---

40. Interview, Marcello.
41. Interview, Donato.
42. Interview, Umberto.
43. Raymond Wolfinger in M. Kent Jennings and L. Harmon Zeigler, *The Electoral Process* (Englewood Cliffs, N. J.: Prentice-Hall, 1966), pp. 42–52.
44. Edward H. Litchfield, *Voting Behavior in a Metropolitan Area* (Ann Arbor, Michigan: University of Michigan Press, 1941).
45. Gunnar Myrdal, *An American Dilemma* (New York: Harper, 1944), p. 435.

emergency. In December 1969, following months of stormy protests by home-owners in Queens over the planned construction of a school, Mayor Lindsay, with an eye for the political support of the Queens residents, removed the chairman of the planning commission and appointed an Italo-American.[46]

The relationship of political strength and distribution of rewards becomes more important with residential segregation, since issues like welfare, crime, and the like become ethnically related matters. If, as I contend, an Italian substructure need not have an ecological base, then the transfer of such ethnically related issues takes place with movement to the suburbs. Some of the rewards and services of local government in particular lead to group patronage; i.e., certain rewards go to a member of a group rather than to the individual.[47] Since the positions at stake involve higher status rather than economic motives, the Italians' quest for rewards becomes instead a quest for a go-between and intermediary. The intermediary will serve as protector and as a symbolic recognition of the Italians' worth and dignity.[48] In a sense, the selection of John Volpe as United States Secretary of Transportation was for this purpose. At the same time the intermediary is used for political purposes. In October of 1970 Volpe appeared before an Italian-American dinner honoring him. His other mission was to show his support for the Republican candidate, Nelson Gross. Referring to the issues of disorder and permissiveness in America, Volpe went on to say that many in his audience, like himself were brought up by Italian-American parents "who were not afraid to use a little discipline."[49]

Ward politics has had both an integrative and disintegrative effect on ethnic groups. Ward politics made the new

46. *New York Times*, October 19, 1969, pp. 1, 72.
47. *Ibid.*, p. 49.
48. Banfield, *City Politics*, pp. 41–43.
49. *Newark Evening News*, October 7, 1970, p. 15. John Volpe employed ethnic appeals in much the same manner in 1972.

arrival aware perhaps for the first time that he was an Italian. By bargaining among the representatives of ethnic groups, the ward politician helped create a sense of community identification.[50] He then turned this identification to his advantage. While integrative in itself, ward politics helped to create wider identifications.[51] Ward politics became disintegrative in that they tended to keep issues on a local rather than on a city-wide basis.

New York City Government may in one sense be viewed, in Banfield's term, as an arbiter, whose task is to manage conflict among competing interests and a heterogeneous population. Political leaders depend on a broad coalition of supporters. Political machines arbitrate internally among the ethnic groups on which they are based and externally among the interests that compete to influence public policies.[52] The political machine was one of the most significant politicizing forces for the Italian. In politics the ethnic leader was able to convert his ethnicity into a positive advantage.[53] The Italians, as do other ethnic groups, represent votes. While we must discount the machine today as the major factor drawing the Italian to the political arena, other factors play their part. Identification with a political leader who is an Italian is still a potent influence, as noted in earlier pages. A political party that achieves recognition and prestige for the Italian is able to draw support for years to come.[54] The party name itself becomes part of the "ethnic ethnocentric pattern of identification." The Italian loyalties, which had been Democratic in the thirties, switched to become Republican because of the war, but swung back again

50. Banfield, *City Politics*, pp. 50–51.
51. Humbert Nelli, "John Powers and the Italians: Politics in a Chicago Ward 1896–1921," *Journal of American History* (June 1970), pp. 67–84.
52. Banfield, *City Politcs*, pp. 50–51. See also Daniel Gordon, "Immigrants and Urban Governmental Form in American Cities," *AJS* 74 (September 1968): 158–71.
53. Nelli, pp. 67–84. See also Oscar Handlin, *Boston's Immigrants*, p. 210.
54. Elmer Cornwall, "Party Absorption of Ethnic Groups: The Case of Rhode Island," *Social Forces* 38 (March 1960): 205–10.

in 1948 and 1952.[55] In Staten Island the Italians drifted into the Republic party following the LaGuardia victory and a growing awareness by the Republicans of the Italian vote potential.

Italians have also been mobilized by intermediary leaders. Predominantly Italian leadership patterns have in the past been molded by the Italians' occupational choices and the social organization of the Italians. The concentration of Italian leadership in building and constructing, with its close political ties, has led to the political arena. For the Italians, the undertaker is often an important political person in the community, with leisure for politics and the incentives to operate a regulated trade.[56] In fact, the candidate to whom I will refer later aroused an interest among our respondents, and he was an undertaker by profession.

As for other ethnic groups, the union has served as an important vehicle for Italian-American political action. The Italians in certain locals of the teamsters and sanitation department unions have tended to mix ethnic politics with union politics. Labor unions in trades where Italians have been concentrated have politicized them because of mutually reinforcing ethnic, occupational, and class interests.

What effect has assimilation had on political participation? Mailey has concluded,

> Italian political recognition blossomed with Roosevelt and by the end of World War II Italians in Philadelphia were turning a deaf ear to ethnic solidarity. As one intelligent political leader put it, "It lost its punch with the war." Many Italians feel that the Italians would suffer in the long run if they continue to assert their background too long. . . . In Philadelphia they feel that the ethnic appeal can only be afforded by Italians who are a large part of the electorate as in New York. Otherwise, the Italians wish to assimilate quickly and make demands for political rewards on another basis.[57]

---

55. See Hugo V. Mailey, "The Italian Vote in Philadelphia Between 1928 and 1946," *POQ* (Spring 1950) , pp. 48–57.
56. Whyte, p. 202.
57. Mailey, pp. 48–57.

Structural assimilation, as I have held, does not diminish ethnicity, because it really has not taken place. Assimilation on some levels may mean a shift in the psychological basis of participation, but not necessarily an increase or decrease in its political salience. The elimination of one motive may make room for others. Assimilated ethnics may develop stronger socioeconomic class interests and political loyalties on this basis. Litchfield found that "insofar as participation is concerned, there is greater solidarity among economic than ethnic and race groups," but while this is true of native whites, it is only tenuously true for ethnic groups.[58] The rank-and-file ethnic who is assimilating may find himself caught between two worlds and may withdraw into apathy, as Child says the second-generation Italian has often done.[59] Wolfinger contends that ethnic politics tended to make economic and social issues less relevant in party competition by emphasizing nationality group rather than social class. By structuring politics so that expectations are for recognition rather than substantive concerns, ethnic strategies divert away from substantive demands.[60] Glazer and Moynihan differ and hold that, because the ethnic group has distinctive economic characteristics, ethnicity becomes a way of referring to social class without appealing to class distinctions.[61]

We have earlier considered the nature of ethnic group conflict in the American political system. With the current discussion of ethniclass, the future configuration of American politics under advanced industrialization becomes a major question. What is suggested by some is the demise of political conflicts implicit in social class itself. Some researchers argue that advanced industrialism has led to a

---

58. Edward Litchfield, *Voting Behavior in a Metropolitan Area* (Ann Arbor, Mich.: University of Michigan Press, 1941), pp. 25–26.
59. Irwin Child. *Italian or American?*, (New Haven, Conn.: Yale University Press, 1943).
60. Jennings, *The Electoral Process*.
61. *Ibid.*

reduction of political conflict because class conflict has subsided as a result of economic expansion and a gradual movement toward equalitarian distribution of rewards.[62] In contrast to this view, Janowitz and Segal argue that while class distinctions may no longer account for the full range of political conflict, new cleavages have emerged in industrial society with the result that conflicts are "manifested by new and more differentiated social groupings" and interests. Thus, a more heterogeneous basis for conflict is laid as new sources of cleavages are opened to interact complexly with the old.[63]

Religion might be considered one of the possible sources of cleavages in society. As a system of beliefs, it defines such notions as justice and what is real in human existence. As a result, the schisms between competing religious systems, or the internal tensions of one religion, become translated into the terminology of political conflict.

In the past the conceptualizations of political conflict generally have centered almost exclusively around social class. Many studies have indicated that religion plays a more active role in the formation of conflicts, and that it does so somewhat independently of social class.[64] The religious factor may be as efficient as social class in predicting political preferences.[65]

Class status, as I have tried to indicate elsewhere, might be indicated by objective criteria as income, education, occupation, residence, the network of social relation, and a person's perception of his own place in society.[66] Political interests for present purposes are designated leftist, centrist,

62. Lawrence E. Hazelrigg, "Religious and Class Bases of Political Conflict in Italy," *AJS* 75 (January 1970) : 497.

63. *Ibid.*

64. Gehart Saenger, "Social Status and Political Behavior," *AJS* (March 1945), pp. 103–13. See also Paul Lazarsfeld *et al. The People's Choice* (New York: Duell, Sloan and Pearce, 1944) .

65. Gehard Lenski, *The Religious Factor* (New York: Doubleday, 1963), pp. 139, 324–27.

66. Lane, *Political Life,* p. 220.

or rightist, according to the respondent's view of his own political outlook. I noted earlier that the degree of associational involvement in the Church, as determined by the extent and frequency of participation in the Church's rituals (i.e., religious involvement), is used as the designation of religious status. Our query was trichotomized to yield strict, moderate, and marginal categories.[67] We found that as we moved from the immigrant group, which we found to be strict Catholics, the ties with the Catholic Church became more tenuous as one moved across the generational span. First-generation respondents remained strict Catholics, those of the second were moderate, and those of the third generation were marginal Catholics. When we correlated this with the respondents' ideological preference, the strict Catholics (i.e., the immigrants) and the first-generation respondents identified with rightist politics as conservatives on local politics. The second-generation, moderate Catholics identified with centrist or moderate politics.[68] The marginal Catholics of the third generation identified with leftist or liberal politics on the local level. On a local political level we find a positive correlation between a strict to marginal religious orientation, and a conservative to liberal political one across the generation span, with movement of Italians from the lower to higher socioeconomic status categories. Variations in religious involvement influence the probability of rightist, centrist, and leftist political choices. Social class distinctions relate to the entire range of political interests. Lower SES (socioeconomic status) Italians, I would predict, would incline toward rightist politics on the local political level. Thus, in local politics, the influence of religion becomes a significant determinant in ideological preference. The evidence seems to indicate a growing polarization of political interests between centrist and rightist position on the one

67. See chapter 3, above; Hazelrigg, "Religious and Class Bases of Conflict in Italy."
68. Question #88. How would you describe yourself—liberal, moderate, conservative?

hand, and the left on the other. This cleavage is owing to the conflicts and tensions of the class structure. A lack of structural assimilation is one dimension of these conflicts and tensions in the class structure. Another source of cleavage related to social class is religion, which touches the lives of people of every class. Liston Pope's observation regarding the relationship between religion and class appears to remain valid:

> Religion despite the close association of its institutions with the class structure is neither simply a product nor a curse, a sanction nor an enemy, of social stratification. It may be either or both as it has been in various societies at various times.[69]

Religion will probably continue for the most part to adapt to class divisions in the United States, and may even intensify them. Religious divisions may become more important indices of stratification.[70] Historically, the internal differentiation in the Catholic Church follows ethnic lines. With the attempt at transplanting his way of life, the immigrant in America sought to reestablish the Church. The ethnic church served to keep alive the identity of Italians. It served as a means to organize themselves and preserve their group identity. The first formally organized structure of the ethnic communities was the church, since it was the source of sacred values and national attitudes. As Warner and Srole have noted,

> The ethnic groups in Yankee City are within a social system that demands conformity on all its sectors, and secures it both by its positive prizes of class mobility and by its negative constraints on the deviant within it. The church structure to an ethnic group threatened with loss of identity serves more than

---

69. Liston Pope, "Religion and Class Structure," *The Annals* (March 1948), p. 91.
70. *Ibid.*, p. 89. Differentiation in Protestantism tends to correspond closely to class differences. Individual Protestant Churches tend to be class churches, with members drawn principally from one class group.

any other structure to organize the group as a community system.[71]

As the number of foreign-born declines in the United States, the nationality churches will lose their peculiar ethnic connections.

Conclusion

Ethniclass serves as an important referent for Italians. The Italian subsociety is linked by class and Italian-American institutions, friendships, structures, and identifications. The units of the subsociety are localized in space in particular communities.

In spite of the loss of an ecological base, the Italian subsociety persists. The movement to the suburbs has not meant the destruction of the Italian subsociety; moreover, in this movement the Italian-American brings with him institutions and in-group social patterns. In addition, those Italians who were most segregated in the central city are the most concentrated in the suburbs. Greater affluence does not lead to the destruction of the subsociety, but allows the maintenance of parallel social structures. The persistence of an Italian-American identification is because such an identity gives him meaning in a mass society where individual identity is lost.

Ethniclass membership then becomes an important stimulus influencing the perceptions of Italian-Americans. In fact, it also serves as part of the Italian-American's perceptual screen.

The lack of structural assimilation leads to the persistence of the Italian subsociety; therefore it leads to the persistence of ethnicity. A structural separation is reflected in the absence of the Italian-American as a group in the higher oc-

---

71. Warner and Srole, p. 218.

cupational, residential, and income categories. Individual mobility in these categories is less a result of group advancement than part of the overall condition of the American economic scene.

The American political system serves to encourage the persistence of an Italian identification because of the continual reliance on ethnic strategies and the fact that ethnic clusters do in fact exist. Out-group rejection leads to a certain uneasiness, which can be ameliorated only by individual or group advancement. Hence, the Italian has a stake in the politics of recognition. The limited number of rewards leads to interethnic conflict. As the rewards at stake involve higher status rather than economic motives, the Italians' quest for rewards becomes a quest for an intermediary who will serve as protector and as a symbolic recognition of the Italians' worth and dignity.

The lack of structural assimilation makes ethnicity take on increased importance in the perceptions and responses of Italian-Americans, particularly on the local level.

Religion becomes a major determinant of ideological orientation in local politics. Strict Catholics, primarily among the immigrants and first-generation respondents, tend to incline to conservative positions. Marginal Catholics, especially of the third generation, incline to the liberal position, while moderate Catholics tend to follow centrist politics in local politics.

5

Political Powerlessness among Italian-Americans

The interaction of several historical developments—the legacy of Rome, the role of the Church, a communal tradition, foreign invasions, a centralized administration, the legacy of the Holy Roman Empire, and the advent of Marxism—has resulted in an imperfect national integration of Italians. These developments have served to produce a society of inner antagonism. These features of the Italian political culture are internalized as individual predispositions.

A sense of powerlessness is greatest through the second generation, but declines (though it is not eliminated) in the third generation. A sense of political powerlessness will be associated with feelings that the political processes do not involve, and have no impact on, the respondent. Moreover, the individual feels that he cannot influence the government in any meaningful way.

The politically alienated individual will tend to be in the younger age categories, possess a low level of education, come from a small city, and have a manual type of occupation.

Ethnic group membership and identification with that group is more strongly associated with a high sense of political powerlessness than among nonethnics.

The Historic Variable

La Palombara has said of Italy:

> The striking truth about Italy is that, except at a superficial level, the leaders of the country have failed to "make Italians."[1]

When we consider the historical variables that have operated to produce political alienation in Italy, an imperfect national integration assumes major importance.

Italy did not emerge as a national state until 1870 for a variety of reasons. The first contributing factor was the inheritance of its Roman past.[2] Rome in Italian history does not stand for Italy but for a much wider concept. It took into its empire a great diversity of land and peoples. Its law and language served as the roads of unification of a vast domain. Even with the fall of the Empire, the ideal of universality lingered on. The Holy Roman Empire was neither Holy nor Roman; neither was it a nation or empire, and the long connection between its chief component parts, Germanic and Italian, was on the whole to work to their mutual disadvantage. The Roman ideal of universality, as it survived the many centuries, was to be a major obstacle to the creation of Italians. Although Rome ruled a vast domain, it was unable to rule the peninsula. The pattern of

---

1. Joseph La Palombara, "Italy: Fragmentation, Isolation, Alienation," in Lucian Pye, *Political Culture and Political Development* (Princeton: Princeton University Press, 1965) , chapter 8, pp. 282-329.
2. René Albrecht-Carrie, *Italy From Napoleon to Mussolini* (New York: Columbia University Press, 1950) , pp. 5-9. See also Dennis Mack Smith. *The Making of Italy 1796-1870* (New York: Walker and Co., 1968) .

jealousies, ambitions, feuds, and rivalries persisted.[3]

The Church became a second obstacle to national integration. The Pope was to operate in a dual capacity following the fall of Rome, as a petty temporal leader and as the representative of a universal idea. The Church became more firmly entrenched in Rome with its claim to temporal power.

A third major obstacle is the communal tradition. In the anarchy that was characteristic of Europe following the fall of Rome, the emergence of city life coincided with the revival of foreign trade. Italian cities were the primary beneficiaries of this revival. As Albrecht-Carrie notes:

> The communal tradition struck deep roots in Italy; it became in fact a much more real and strong, because living, force than the remote and embalmed influence of old Rome herself. . . . [P]recisely because this was a force of such vitality and one that commanded intense loyalty, it led after a while to a process of crystallization that prevented the grasping of the broader horizon of a larger unity.[4]

Localism or parochialism is still in evidence in Italy today. There are frequent hostilities among many cities. Recently, violence erupted when a provincial capital was changed from one city to another in southern Italy.[5]

A fourth impulse, which was to leave enduring marks on Italian society, was the succession of foreign invasions.[6] What is important to mention here is not the long list of such events, but that the country was never rescued from the necessity of relying on regimes, protectors, or guardians to prevent civil wars, revolutions, and invasions. Salvadori writes,

It is difficult to say which of the two main developments of

---

3. Robert Ardrey, *The Territorial Imperative* (New York: Dell Publishing Co., 1966) , p. 184.
4. Albrecht-Carrie, p. 9.
5. *New York Times*, October 17, 1970. The capital was changed from Reggio Calabria to Catanzaro.
6. Smith, *The Making of Italy 1796–1870.*

the sixteenth century in Italy—the Great Reformation or the establishment of Spanish domination—had the greater influence in moulding the contemporary nation. The two developments helped each other. They combined to produce conformity, deviousness, docility; to create the conviction that governmental authority is beyond the reach of common people, that the hierarchical order is the natural order.[7]

Barzini also observes the impact of foreign rule on individual behavior,

> He is powerless to deflect the tides of history. He can only try to defend himself from their blind violence, keep his mouth shut and mind his own business.[8]

> They behave with circumspection, caution and even cynicism. . . .
> They know the world is an ugly and pitiless place, and adapt themselves, without useless recriminations to its inviolable laws.[9]

Even the Italian unification movement was never a mass movement. It did not attract the average Italian, but rather the northern middle and upper classes.[10] The Italy that emerged was not the Italy desired by either Mazzini or Garibaldi.[11] The nation began its life without the widespread participation of the masses, with only the half-hearted support of the people south of Rome, and the opposition of the Catholic Church, which was outraged over the loss of its power.[12]

Still another obstacle to national integration was the centralized administration system imposed by Piedmont, which

7. Massimo Salvadori, *Italy* (Englewood Cliffs, N. J.: Prentice Hall, 1965), p. 89.
8. Luigi Barzini, *The Italians* (New York: Atheneum, 1965), p. 157.
9. *Ibid.,* p. 165.
10. Smith, pp. 323–35. See also Eric Whelpton, *A Concise History of Italy* (New York: Roy Publishers, 1964), pp. 174–83.
11. Smith, pp. 214–27, 307–23. See also Albrecht-Carrie, pp. 31–36.
12. Albrecht-Carrie, p. 7. See also Raymond Grew, "The Church in Italian Life," *Symposium on Modern Italy: Columbia University* (November 1969).

served to deny Italians the very experience with political participation it sorely needed.[13] In exchange for a central government, the South was left pretty much to itself. Piedmont was able to "buy" the support of the southern "notables" who saw their region as a place to exploit for personal gain, and not as an area to develop.[14] Thus, the south began its experience in the new nation under a policy of neglect and corruption typical of Bourbon administrators. Few of the post-unification leaders from Piedmont went as far south as Rome. Southern Italy was regarded for some time as an area of natural riches. Later, when this view was finally not borne out by the facts, its backwardness was attributed to the inherent backwardness and inferiority of the southern Italian. For the south, unification was to become a liability. It was to bear a disproportionate amount of taxes.[15]

The Church and the great material power of the Holy Roman Empire made a durable alliance, which lasted from the sack of Rome until September 1870.[16] This alliance preserved a splendid, but corrupt and humiliating, peace.[17] The Holy Roman Church also opposed the creation of a united Italy, which led to the papal prohibition against Catholic participation in the affairs of the new nation. For fifty years the Church kept its adherents isolated from participation. When it lifted the ban, it was because of the fear of the growing forces of Socialism. Catholicism since the end of World War II has been the dominant force in Italian politics.[18] The Church came to be viewed as weighted

---

13. Albrecht-Carrie, pp. 36–43.
14. Dennis Mack Smith, *Italy: A Modern History* (Ann Arbor, Mich.: University of Michigan Press, 1969).
15. *Ibid.*
16. Luigi Barzini, "Italy: The Fragile State," *Foreign Affairs* (April 1968), p. 564.
17. A. C. Jemolo, *Church and State in Italy 1850–1950* (Oxford: Beauchurd, 1960). See also Grew, "The Church in Italian Life."
18. Jemolo, *Church and State.* See also R. A. Webster, *The Cross and the Fasces: Christian and Fascism in Italy* (Stanford, Calif.: University of California Press, 1960).

down by the past and tied inextricably to it, rather than as a dynamic force seeking to meet the needs of the Italian people. The Church became so imbedded in politics that the Christian Democrats and the Church were almost synonymous. The Christian Democratic party recognized its dependence on the Church for a popular base, yet it would somehow have to cut its bonds with traditionalism and clericalism if it was to compete in a relevant way on social issues. In the years since the end of the War, its political intervention was justified on the basis of the threat to it represented by Marxism.

The advent of Marxism in Italy, under the conditions that existed in the country, served to make left-wing thought and attitudes toward existing institutions take on a more extreme slant. Italy was filled with a variety of Marxism that molded a basically antagonistic and alienative attitude toward politics and the state.[19]

Centuries of political fragmentation, inadequate communication, a succession of invasions by foreign and competing powers, and a strong local political and cultural tradition served as factors in perpetuating an imperfect political integration. Added to these are a long history of poverty, illiteracy, and injustice, particularly in the Mezzogiorno (the south). Italy has been influenced by historical occurrences, crises, and conditions that have served to fractionalize rather than to cement the political system, and to intensify rather than to diminish the sense of divisiveness that is necessary to achievement of national integration.[20]

Political Powerlessness

It is important to note at this point that this approach to political alienation is different from other attempts to clarify the concept, in that it focuses on the perceptions,

---

19. La Palombara, p. 302.
20. Ardrey, pp. 183, 187.

held by Italians across a three-generation span, referring to the institutions of government and the political process. In a certain respect, this approach holds constant the institutional referent of alienation by dealing with individual perceptions.

Political alienation, as employed in this study, is the rejection by the individual of the dominant roles, values, and institutions of society based upon a real or perceived exclusion of the individual from the political processes of society by other individuals, groups, or the power arrangements in that society.[21] Political alienation has four components:[22]

1. Political powerlessness may be defined as an individual's feeling that he cannot affect the actions of government, that the authoritative allocation of values, which is at the heart of the political process, is not subject to his influence.

2. Political meaninglessness occurs when political decisions are perceived as being unpredictable. This mode of alienation is distinguished from powerlessness in that in the latter, decisions may be predictable, but are not subject to the influence of the individual. Political meaninglessness is a situation in which the individual perceives no discernible pattern. Thus, the individual is unable to distinguish any meaningful political choices.

3. Political normlessness is defined as the individual's perception that the norms or rules intended to govern political

---

21. Kenneth Keniston, *The Uncommitted Youth: Alienated Youth in American Society* (New York: Harcourt, Brace & World, Inc., 1966), p. 454. This is an adaptation of Kenniston's definition. While political alienation is an individual perception it may have objective reality in that the institutional structure of the society may seek to exclude a type of person or group.

22. Ada Finfiter, "Dimensions of Political Alienation," *APSR* (June 1970), pp. 390–91. The specification of the ways that political alienation is expressed is based entirely on Finfiter's discussion of this subject. See Angus Campbell, Philip Converse, Warren Miller, and Donald Stokes, *The American Voter* (New York: John Wiley, 1960). This mode of alienation, i.e., powerlessness, is related to the concept of political efficiency which has concerned so many including Campbell, et al.

relations have broken down, and that departures from prescribed behavior are common.

4. Political isolation refers to a rejection of political norms
and goals that are widely held and shared by other members
of society.[23] We will attempt to explore political alienation
among Italians along two of these dimensions—political
powerlessness and political normlessness.[24] Barzini com-
mented on the relationship between power and the individual:

> all of the official institutions are weak and unstable in Italy;
> the law is flexible and unreliable, the State is discredited and
> easily dominated by powerful persons and groups, and society
> . . . has little influence . . . yet . . . life around them flows
> easily; man is not always devoured by man. . . . Life for re-
> signed and disenchanted people appears to be no more cruel
> than in better organized countries . . . his security depends
> not on the combined exertions of his countrymen to which he

23. The following questions served as an index of political powerlessness.
Question #102. Who do you say runs the government?
Question #104. Suppose a law was being considered by the government that you considered unjust or harmful. What do you think you could
do about it?
Question #106. If you made an effort to change it, would you be
successful?
Question #105. If such a situation arose, how likely is it that you
could do something about it?
Question #109. How much effect does government have on your everyday life?
Question #107. Some people say that there is little use in writing to
a politician since he is not really interested in the problems of the average
person. Do you agree?
Question #127. Does the outcome of an election make any real difference?
Question #101. Some people say that politics and government are so
complicated that the average man can't really understand what is going on.
Do you agree? Why?
Question #100. How well do you understand important national and
international issues?
Question #96. Are there some people with whom you definitely
wouldn't discuss politics?
Question #120. Can you think of any election in which you were
particularly interested?
Question #115. Do you vote regularly? Were there times you didn't
vote?
Question #108. Are strikes of political benefit?
24. My research design was limited to these two dimensions.

should add his own, but mostly on his individual capacities and native shrewdness. . . . [H]e can occupy in society only which-ever position he can conquer and defend with his personal authority. . . . Power, personal power, is the key.[25]

A sense of powerlessness is strongly evident among the Italian immigrants interviewed, and is also evident among the first- and second-generation respondents. There is a major decline in such feelings among the third generation, although some traces still linger.

Most of the immigrants tended to see government, both in Italy and the United States, as being run by forces other than themselves.[26] The forces frequently mentioned were government officials, politicians, unions, or just "the" power-ful. It is interesting to note that government officials were viewed as something apart from an alien to the respondent's aspirations. Rarely were government officials or politicians perceived as representatives. As Lane notes,

> The alienated man not only believes that government is fail-ing to serve his interests; he believes that it is also serving some other set of interests, either those of a rival class of "the vested interests" or some hostile, disliked, rejected group. . . . [T]he political alienate believes that such a group is receiving the awards to be given by a biased government.[27]

Political activity among the immigrants seemed to spring forth principally during election time, which, in fact, took on the aura of people going to listen to speakers or political actors. In their role as spectators to political action, they resembled the spectators at a performance of an opera, a tragic one at that.

Most of the first-, second-, and third-generation respon-dents showed the impact of the American political culture

---

25. Barzini, pp. 187, 189.
26. G. Almond and S. Verba, *The Civic Culture* (Princeton, N. J.: Prince-ton University Press, 1963) , pp. 47–48.
27. Robert Lane, *Political Ideology* (Glencoe, Ill.: The Free Press, 1962) , p. 171.

by viewing the operation of government from the stand-point of intermediaries or representatives. Those represen-tatives, however, may be more responsive to the "more in-fluential," who may be individuals or groups. Paul, a bright-eyed aspiring accountant, in his usual machine-gun-like answers, at first said that it was the representatives who ran the government, but then conditioned this by adding, "who more or less represent the average person. Often it's the most powerful."[28] To Larry, an automotive dealer, the influential were, "Those who have money . . . the higher ups,"[29] while Sal, another second-generation respondent, asserted, "The politicians often disregard the people and cater to special interests."[30] A frequent response in all three groups echoed the view of the moustachioed Mario who burst forth with the contention that the most powerful was, "the overall Wasp establishment."[31] Even Father Andrew, a third-gener-ation respondent, asserted that he would at first mention the representatives, but really it's the more influential and established groups like the Wasps.[32]

Most of the immigrants see all levels of government as having little or no impact on their daily lives. This picture does not change drastically among the first-, second-, and third-generation respondents.[33] When faced with a hypo-thetical situation in which government passed an unjust law, the immigrant respondents felt they could do little to change it.[34] Most, already influenced by the American political system, indicated that groups could be formed for political action. Donato, the bony-faced pattern-maker, affirmed this position, saying, "The individual can do nothing; you need

28. Interview, Paul.
29. Interview, Larry.
30. Interview, Sal.
31. Interview, Mario. I will discuss the implications of core culture domi-nation in my conclusion.
32. Interview, Father Andrew.
33. Almond and Verba, p. 51.
34. Ibid.

a group,"[35] while Umberto was less optimistic, declaring, "You could do little, only express your opinion."[36] Alfredo, a draftsman, was typical of the immigrants' estimation of their success in changing the situation, asserting, "It depends if you have the right people helping . . . you need help from the higher-ups. You can't fight city hall. You must have the right key to the government. You've got to have power."[37] The majority of the immigrants felt that the success of a group's efforts depended on the numbers involved, and even if this factor existed, they were less than optimistic about changing things.[38]

The pattern on the whole does not change drastically among the first-generation respondents. Most of them listed lower forms of political activity in possibly changing the "unjust law." Most of them were not optimistic of their success. Paul conditioned his "possible success," stating, "It depends on who your opponent was. If it was a powerful economic interest, particularly of a large business, you can forget it. Many of the economic interests use their money for campaign contributions and outright bribes to influence a government decision."[39] Mario, a young lawyer, suggested extra-legal means. "It's not likely by normal means. There are few local issues which excite a large number of people. One would have to use more radical means, such as disrupting a meeting. This gets results."[40]

Both the second- and third-generation respondents shared this pessimism in changing things. While they were more disposed to mention the use of groups, rarely did the respondents suggest the formation of a group. In almost every case, it was a question of joining one already in existence.

---

35. Interview, Donato.
36. Interview, Umberto.
37. Interview, Alfredo.
38. Almond and Verba, p. 51.
39. Interview, Paul.
40. Interview, Mario.

Most in both groups conditioned their political action. Laura, a third-generation student, said that political action depended on the issue, and at that, "I wouldn't go out of my way, only if it affected me directly."[41] Carmen felt similarly, declaring, "If it really interested me, I just might."[42] Even when a lower form of political activity is suggested, such as writing to a government official, nearly all of the immigrants see that action as having little impact on things.[43] The above reinforces an earlier conclusion that southern Italians tend to see government as a thing apart from them, not something involving them. "I don't think he would even read my letter," exclaimed Bruno, the curly-headed factory worker.[44] Alfredo reaffirmed this cynicism: "I think he has his mind already made up."[45] While the first generation seemed to express a little more faith in the effectiveness of writing their representatives, most conditioned the impact of doing so on how many engaged in the same process. Bob, a printer aspiring to get a college education, was more optimistic, claiming, "Yes they will read it and it will have an impact. The My Lai incident was exposed as a result of such a letter. I also saw letters get results when I was in the Air Force."[46] The second generation respondents were positive in their belief in the success of this minimal form of political activity, and most did not think its success depended on large numbers of people doing the same thing. Sal dissented from this optimism, declaring, "No, it will not be read; they won't listen. Lobbyists are too powerful. They dispense bribes and money to influence government. People have no influence; it's all a matter of how much money one makes. The politicians are not really worried about people."[47] This skepticism emerges even more strongly

41. Interview, Laura.
42. Interview, Carmen.
43. Almond and Verba, p. 51.
44. Interview, Bruno.
45. Interview, Alfredo.
46. Interview, Bob.
47. Interview, Sal.

among the third-generation respondents as Laura said, disgustedly, "On the whole, they would not pay attention except near election time."[48]

Most of the immigrants tended to see politics and government as too complicated to really understand.[49] According to the respondents, various factors accounted for this. To Donato it is because "too many deals take place,"[50] while Mina, a secretary, said, "The problem is, who is or what is the government." Umberto, who had a burning interest in computers, said almost with annoyance, "I have too many things on my mind. I don't know who to really believe,"[51] while Bruno reaffirmed this view exasperatedly, with "It's very confusing. Only those who are really or actually involved truly understand it."[52]

This view did not change among the first- and second-generation respondents. Bob attributed it to "school did a poor job of educating in politics,"[53] while Mario, another first-generation respondent, looked to politics in general: "The average person sees politics as made up of a series of lies and corrupt people."[54] Sal is representative of the second-generation view and asserts in the same vein that "it's complicated because of the way they do business. They are not honest. They tell people one thing and already are thinking about the ways to get around what they just said. Politics is a whore's game."[55]

It is interesting to note that the third-generation respondents still perceived politics as being complicated, but the reasons shift. Father Andrew is typical of them: "Government doesn't make the effort of making things clearer for

---

48. Interview, Laura.
49. Almond and Verba, p. 50. See also David Abbott, *Political Alienation in Italy and Mexico* (Ph.D. dissertation, University of North Carolina, 1966), pp. 117–19. Levin, pp. 58–75.
50. Interview, Donato.
51. Interview, Umberto.
52. Interview, Bruno.
53. Interview, Bob.
54. Interview, Mario.
55. Interview, Sal.

the citizen. There's a lack of caring for the citizen. But even if this is the case, the burden is on the citizen to find out what is going on. He has to make the effort."[56] Thus, the reason behind assigning blame for bad or remote government shifts from the respondents' general conception of politics or of specific political actors to individual apathy or noninvolvement.

Along with this view of the complicated nature of politics is a low level of political information among immigrants. It remains low-to-average among the first- and second-generation respondents.[57] Interestingly enough, however, while there is a low level of political information, there is less reluctance to discuss politics with other people. As one proceeds to the higher levels of perceived understanding, especially among the third-generation respondents, there is greater reluctance to discuss politics, particularly with people who hold opposite views from theirs. There seems to be an increasing quest for reinforcement of views, to a point perhaps of political conformity with others of the same outlook.

Most of the immigrants interviewed tended to have little interest in elections, although the overwhelming number had voted regularly in Italy.[58] As one proceeds across the three-generational span, the level of interest increases. Noninterest is usually expressed in terms of specific elections. While regularity of voting behavior is characteristic of all three generations, the respondents in all groups nevertheless saw the act of voting as it related to the outcome of an election as not making any difference. This pattern continues as one moves from the immigrant group to the third generation. Many agreed with Vincent that it would make a difference: "If the candidates campaign on different and

---

56. Interview, Father Andrew.
57. Almond and Verba, pp. 169–73, 237. See also Abbott, p. 109.
58. Georgio Galli and Alfonso Prandi, *Patterns of Political Participation in Italy* (New Haven: Yale University Press, 1970), pp. 28–29.

distinct policies, liberal and conservative positions."[59] Lou held that "in the long run it will have an effect, but not for the short run. This kind of impact will depend on different policies, since the Liberal will certainly pass one kind of program while the Conservative another."[60]

Demographic Variables of Political Alienation

The sample of respondents is not large enough for one to reach definite conclusions as to the age and sex variables of the politically alienated. However, it does offer conditional statements with regard to the proportion of the respondents who are politically alienated along sex and age lines. It appears that among Italian immigrants there is no significant difference among men and women who are politically alienated. This pattern seems to continue, although I would predict that more women than men across generational lines would tend to feel "more powerless" than men. Men, I would predict, would tend to perceive more normative violations than women.[61]

Among the new arrivals we find an overall pattern of political alienation among those between 18 and 30 years of age, and for the first, second, and third generations, the politically alienated would seem to fall into the 31 to 50 age category.[62] The average age of the politically alienated among all respondents was 30.6. A younger age among the politically alienated Italian immigrants may be explained by the fact that Italian immigration to the United States is becoming increasingly characterized by very high proportions of individuals within this very age group. It may also be explained by the fact that this age group is most acutely aware of the major changes taking place in Italian society. They see the end of the old rural society and the

59. Interview, Vincent.
60. Interview, Lou.
61. Abbott, p. 64.

emergence of an industrial one, and hence refuse to follow their parents' vocation on the land. There is no other work for them in the *paese,* (town) so they flock to the cities. However, they now face the spectre of an impersonal economic and social structure, as well as unemployment. While they are fed up with the old way of life in the town, they are insecure outside its traditions and frustrated with their inability to find a place in the emerging, more complex, industrial life of Italy. Most have dismissed the old aristocrats and bourgeois as exploiters. Most feel the Church is irrelevant and are cynical about the democracy and Christianity of the CDs. As Paulsen notes,

> Underneath all this . . . is a deep anxiety to discover his own niche in life. The years are passing—soon he will be thirty—and every day the town changes. He feels suspended between two worlds: the familiar rural life of his parents, and the lure of a dignified job and the comfort and sophistication of the city. His protest is against his uselessness, his sterile existence, the complete paralysis of the forces of society to help him.[63]

The age grouping of the politically alienated among the first-, second-, and third-generation respondents may be explained by the lower mobility rates than the respondents anticipated, and the realization that cultural assimilation did not bring with it structural assimilation.

Of those politically alienated, the lower the level of education, the higher the proportion of those who felt politically powerless.[64] Less than half of the immigrants had primary or elementary education, whereas the remaining number had education ranging from this level to a university education. Most of the first-, and second-generation respondents had a high school education, while most of those of the third generation had a university education. Among those who advanced up the educational ladder, there was a

---

62. *Ibid.*
63. Paulsen, p. 270.
64. Abbott, pp. 60–61. See Almond and Verba, p. 173.

decreasing sense of political powerlessness, but an increasing sense of political normlessness. Thus, low educational attainment has a relationship to powerlessness, and a higher educational attainment, to political normlessness.

Although the sample is not broad enough to show it, I suggest that those Italian immigrants coming from smaller cities to larger ones would tend to be more politically alienated. This would seem true of the immigrant who has come to a large city environment, and now feels he is dwarfed by the enormity of his new surroundings and is unable to cope with them.[65] For the first-, second-, and third-generation respondents, this movement brings with it a loss of control of political affairs that he may more likely have held in a small-town environment.

I suggested in earlier pages that a perceived sense of exclusion from the dominant roles and institutions of society has some foundation in objective reality. Ethnic group membership and social stratification then loom large as determinants of Italian political alienation. Variations in the feelings of political powerlessness and perceived political normlessness are associated with the individual's position in the social structure, as determined by occupation, income, education, age, and sex. A low perception in the social structure by the Italian in all groups is interpreted as inaccessibility to the means to achieve desired ends, and, therefore, his exclusion from the dominant roles, institutions, and values of society. Italy's closed class system has been characterized above as disjunctive. I have indicated elsewhere that Italy is undergoing changes.

Lopreato's data on occupational mobility in Italy lends support to the Lipset-Bendix hypothesis relating occupational mobility to the level of industrialization.[66] Lipset and Bendix contend that "the social mobility of societies becomes relatively high once their industrialization, and hence

65. Abbott, pp. 71–72.
66. Joseph Lopreato, "Social Mobility in Italy," *AJS* (November 1965).

their economic expansion, reaches a certain level."[67] Lopreato supports their hypothesis that "mobility patterns in Western industrialized societies are determined by the occupational structure," rather than by the political institutions. He found that the rates of upward and downward mobility in Italy are today highly comparable to those found within the past two decades in various other industrialized countries.[68]

As far as the situation in America is concerned, Bernard Rosen holds that upward mobility rates are dissimilar for many racial and ethnic groups.[69] Those people with small-town or urban environment origins were more likely to possess the cultural values appropriate to achievement in American society than those people whose culture was formed in rural peasant surroundings. Rosen tries to show that some persons have a higher need for achievement, while others have a low need for achievement.[70] According to him there are three aspects of the "achievement orientation": 1. "achievement orientation"; 2. "value orientations"; 3. "culturally influenced educational aspiration levels."[71] Rosen then concluded, "As a consequence, achievement motivation is more characteristic of Greeks, Jews, and white Protestants than of Italians, French-Canadians, and Negroes."[72] Thus, Italians have, in Rosen's terms, a "low need for achieve-

---

67. Seymour Martin Lipset and Reinhard Bendix, *Social Mobility in Industrial Society* (Berkeley: University of California Press, 1959) , pp. 13, 73, 24–26.

68. Lopreato, p. 314.

69. Bernard Rosen, "Race, Ethnicity and Achievement Syndrome," *ASR* 24 (October 1959) : 47–60.

70. *Ibid.*, p. 48.

71. As Joseph Lopreato points out with regard to these three aspects, "Equipped with this conceptual scheme, Rosen turned to his students enrolled in two sociology classes who, with instructions never made public, spent their Christmas vacation in sixty-two communities in four states of the Northeast interviewing pairs of mothers and sons belonging to different nationality and racial groups." "Social Science and Achievement Motivation Among Italian-Americans," in Frank Femminella, ed., *Power and Class: The Italian-American Experience Today* (Staten Island, N.Y.: The American-Italian Historical Association, 1973) , pp. 4, 48–49.

72. Rosen, p. 60.

ment." He also found that a great number of Black Americans would be satisfied with even the lowest jobs. This indicated to Rosen a low vocational aspiration.

Lopreato correctly exposes these false assumptions that are the underpinning of Rosen's conceptual scheme and measures of motivation:

> It is hard to understand the "inconsistency" in the behavior of Black Americans was not sufficient to sensitize Mr. Rosen to the deficiencies of his methods. Can you imagine the Black American mother, endlessly accused of not raising her children to honor the American Dream, not telling interviewer "Joe College" that she "intended" to send her son to school as long as everyone did? . . . But judiciousness is in short supply in our science; or as far as Italian-Americans are concerned, Rosen might have wondered whether, according to such things as census materials, his research tool had much predictive power at all.[73]

Lopreato proposes that what hard-working, deprived people actually achieve is somehow a better measure of their potential for achievement than the methodology of some social scientists, which often says more about "the personality and the ideology of the inquirers than about the achievement potential of the interviewed."[74]

Italians were found by Fred Strodtbeck to be less mobile than Jews in New Haven. Strodtbeck found that both Italian and Jewish boys generally guessed that their parents would be satisfied if they chose high-status positions, but it was predominantly the Italian boys who also thought that their parents would be pleased with less. In his study, the Italians were found to be more accepting of lower-status occupations.[75] Strodtbeck supports Rosen's findings of low achievement among Italians of New Haven, which is due

73. *Ibid.,* p. 6.
74. *Ibid.,* p. 7.
75. Fred Strodtbeck, Margaret McDonald and Bernard Rosen, "Evaluation of Occupation: A Reflection of Jewish and Italian Mobility Differences," *ASR* 22 (October 1957) : 546–53.

to "culturally influenced educational-vocational aspiration levels," and concludes, "To the typical southern Italian peasant, school was an upper-class institution and potentially a threat to his desire to retain his family life about him. . . ."[76] Rosen and Strodtbeck's explanation of the apparent low achievement implies a certain antagonism toward school or of "intellectualism," which was regarded with distrust. This explanation is not only inaccurate but misleading. As Lopreato notes, "The peasants distrusted—and they still distrust—intellectuals for their constant abuses, not intellectualism or learning per se."[77] Early southern Italian immigrants did have certain attitudes about the formal American educational institutions, which need clarification. They did perceive correctly that the school and teachers in that era were hostile to the family. Many did not see the value of the education provided by the American high school of that period. In school, Italian children were advised to train for manual, working-class occupations. Many educators judged that they lacked the mental endowments necessary for other occupations.[78] The Italian families, sensing this, felt that the trades could be learned more readily and more expertly on the job while the youngster was being paid at the same time.

The American schools held the immigrants and their culture in contempt. This middle-class institution then effectively produced a "rebel" type of reaction against it and parental authority, especially as the child became more successful. The southern Italian immigrant sensed quite perceptively that the school with its Americanizationist and absorptionist thrust would soon strip him and his family of their identity.[79] Lopreato observes, "The tendency to

76. Fred L. Strodtbeck, "Family Interaction, Values, and Achievement," in Marshall Sklare, ed., *The Jews: Social Patterns of an American Group* (New York: Free Press, 1958), p. 150.

77. Joseph Lopreato, *Italian-Americans* (New York: Random House, 1970), p. 154.

78. This is a not uncommon practice today in many urban schools.

79. Lopreato, *Italian-Americans*, p. 160.

compare Italian-Americans to especially successful groups to suggest, however, unintentionally, that Italians are poor achievers is patently unwarranted by the facts."[80] The success of some groups can't be explained in terms of greater achievement motivation or a greater reverence for learning. Regardless of ethnic background, individuals "will set those goals that are highly valued in their society and appear to be attainable given their past experience with success and the means presently at their disposal."[81] Lopreato suggests that what may be more to the point is not that Italians are "under-achievers" but rather that some of these other groups may be "over-achievers."[82]

It is wrong or inaccurate to assume that cultural achievement results solely from mental powers and therefore, that some people or groups want to get ahead more than others. "Rather, it seems obvious that, in addition to the questions of differential access to existing avenues to success, different people have different strategies and time schedules for the attainment of the same goals."[83] Hence, the overemphasis on motivation and need for achievement does not take into consideration the unequal distribution of opportunities or what is achievable, but reflects "a preoccupation with 'the rat race' that, if what certain sections of our youth today believe is true, empties man too much of his human content."[84]

Manual occupations seem to predominate among the immigrant respondents, while nonmanual ones seem increasingly to predominate as one moves from the first to the third generation.[85] Manual occupations are associated with political alienation. However, manual occupations prevail most strongly among the immigrants and first-generation respondents, declining gradually in the second generation. The

80. *Ibid.,* p. 164.
81. *Ibid.,* p. 165.
82. *Ibid.* pp. 164–65.
83. *Ibid.,* p. 165.
84. *Ibid.*
85. Abbott, pp. 59, 62. See also chapter 3, above.

association of manual occupations with high political alienation is explainable by the prevalence of the feeling that
the individual is unable to control the work environment.[86]
I have reported previously on the income levels of the
respondents. The income level increased gradually from the
immigrant to the third generation, but only two of all respondents could be considered in the moderate upper-income bracket.[87] Thus, low income levels among the respondents are positively correlated with high political powerlessness.

Conclusions

This study yielded no information to indicate that the
Italian immigrant or Italian-American is anomic. The
American political system does not appear to increase or
decrease personal normlessness among either of these two
groups. There was no clear correlation between personal
mistrust and political alienation.

The southern Italian family provides its members with
no coherent view of the national political system. The decision-making process in the southern Italian family does
not prepare its members to take part in democratic political
structures. As the family structure is altered in the direction
of shared decision-making among its members, there is a
decline in political powerlessness and personal normlessness.

Those respondents whose occupational positions were drastically lower than parental or personal aspirations were more
likely to feel politically powerless. This result was strongest
up to the second generation. Those respondents whose oc-

---

86. A. G. Neal and S. Retigg, "Dimensions of Alienation Among Manual
and Non-Manual Workers," *ASR* (August 1963), pp. 599–608.

87. According to the 1970 census figures, educational attainment among
Italian-Americans between the ages of 24 and 34 is equal to that of the
nation as a whole—12.5 years of school. Higher educational attainment however, is not reflected in massive entry on the part of Italian-Americans into
the higher-income and occupational categories. See William Aho, "Ethnic
Mobility in Northeastern United States," *The Sociological Quarterly* 10 (Fall
1969) : 512–26.

cupational positions were the same or lower than those of their parents were more likely to feel politically powerless.

Marginal Catholics, who appeared most frequently among the third-generation Italian-Americans, were associated with high perceived normlessness, while moderate Catholics, who appeared most often among the first and second generation, were associated with high political powerlessness.

A person of the same ethniclass, that is, a low socioeconomic status, and Italian-American group membership is associated with high political powerlessness. This relationship was seen to remain constant until the third generation, where a decline in political powerlessness and a relative increase in political normlessness was noted. Religion, ethnic group membership, and social class are strong determinants in this development.

The decline in political powerlessness in the third generation may be explained by a higher educational attainment and the relative advance into the higher income and occupational hierarchies, even though it is not to the degree or at the rate desired by the respondents.[88] Those with greater knowledge of the political system, which, one presumes, increases with educational attainment, would be more apt to perceive the norm deviations that do, in fact, occur, than those to whom the political structure is less familiar. Third-generation respondents probably have the highest expectations regarding the behavior of public officials, rooted in an idealized orientation toward government and authority common in public schooling. Violations of this image may evoke negative responses. The political culture of Italy tends to stress a realistic and more cynical image of government. As Barzini says of the Italians, "They learned long ago . . . to be sober and clear-eyed, realistic in all circumstances." With lower expectations they may tend to be more tolerant of what they may perceive to be the far less frequent occurrence of norm violations in their adopted country.

88. Finfiter, p. 400.

6

Political Normlessness among Italian-Americans

Italian-Americans who are of the lower socioeconomic categories and are moderate Catholics are strongly associated with feelings of high political powerlessness, but with lower feelings of perceived normlessness than members of the host society.[1] This relationship remains constant through the second generation of Italian-Americans. There is a decline in political powerlessness, though not a sharp or substantial one, among the third-generation Italian-Americans, and a relative increase in perceived political normlessness. An increase in political normlessness relative to political powerlessness may be attributed to those among the third-generation Italian-Americans having higher levels of education. It is assumed that higher educational attainment brings with it greater knowledge of the American political system, hence the identification of norm violations. The persistence

---

1. I am referring to ethniclass.

of these two modes of alienation is attributed to a lack of structural assimilation among Italian-Americans, reflected in their membership in the lower occupational, income, and residential categories.

A higher educational attainment that is not reflected in an improvement in occupational or status position is associated with high political powerlessness. A changed family structure in the direction of shared decision-making within the Italian-American families is reflected in a decline in political powerlessness. In addition, an improvement in occupational position or an increased income as compared to the respondents' parents will also result in a decline in political powerlessness, but not a drastic decline unless the change is a significant improvement either in status or in absolute terms.

Political perceptions may be thought of as having behavioral and attitudinal roots in nonpolitical areas of life. A number of studies have sought to explore this relationship.[2] Some researchers have tried to explain political alienation as an extension of personal or social alienation. Still others have looked at it as the political manifestation of alienation from the work situation in which the individual finds himself.[3] It is the purpose of this chapter to explore the nonpolitical variables as they relate to political alienation.

Horton and Thompson have concluded that political alienation is closely associated with social alienation and interpersonal mistrust.[4] Banfield has found that social mistrust is often generalized by individuals to the political

2. Campbel *et al.*, *The Voter Decides*, chapter 2; T. W. Adorno, Else Frankel Brunswick, Daniel Levinson and R. Nevitt Sanford, *The Authoritarian Personality* (New York: Harper, 1950); Herbert Hyman, *Political Socialization* (Glencoe, Ill.: The Free Press, 1959); Almond and Verba, *The Civic Culture;* Robert Lane, *Political Life,* chapters 7–12.

3. Horton and Thompson, p. 195; Lane, *Political Ideology,* pp. 177–78; Fromm, *The Sane Society;* Blauner, *Alienation and Freedom.*

4. Horton and Thompson, p. 195; Franz Neumann, *The Democratic and the Authoritarian State* (Glencoe, Ill.: The Free Press, 1957), pp. 290–95; William Kornhauser, *The Politics of Mass Society* (Glencoe, Ill.: The Free Press, 1959).

realm.[5] Perceived political normlessness as used here will mean the respondent believes that frequent deviations from accepted norms take place in the political process.[6]

In only three instances did the immigrants feel that the position of the average person was actually getting worse.[7] Donato lamented, "One can never get ahead. Taxes . . . inflation. Once you get to the middle class you can never get out."[8] Most of the first-generation respondents agreed with Bob that, because of technological advances and social benefits, things for the average person were getting better. Among most of the second-generation respondents is found a definite disagreement with the immigrant and first-generation groups. Most attributed the weakened state of affairs for the average person not only to economic factors but to social factors as well. As Sal put it, "With respect to the morale and closeness of people to one another, it has deteriorated because people don't care about anything, only themselves. They're in their own world. Economically they may be better off, but not as 'people.' "[9] This same feeling is evident among the third-generation respondents who, with Laura, felt that the average person was better off economically but not socially: "for example, family life, lawlessness in society, and a self-serving mentality."[10]

When asked if it was better to think of today and forget about tomorrow, there was an overwhelming uniformity across the three-generational span.[11] The immigrants strongly disagreed with the statement. Some, like Alfredo, asserted, "No, I don't agree. This is the American way of thinking.

---

5. Banfield, *The Moral Basis for Backward Society.*
6. I have used five questions as an index of normlessness.
7. Question #30. Some say that the position of the average person is getting worse. Do you agree?
8. Interview, Donato.
9. Interview, Sal.
10. Question #43. Some people say that human nature is fundamentally selfish. Agree—Disagree.
Interview, Laura. See Abbott, p. 82; Almond and Verba, p. 213.
11. Question #31. Some say that it is better to live today and let tomorrow take care of itself. Do you agree?

You must think and plan for tomorrow and for your children."[12] Most of those of the second and third generation felt as Lou did, "I know that many think this way. They have welfare and Uncle Sam, so why think about tomorrow? Let the government take care of tomorrow. I'm not like this."[13] Vincent dissented, saying, "We are too future-oriented. We don't enjoy life. We should live totally each day."[14]

In the dimension of personal trust, there was again a certain uniformity across the three-generational span, viewing human nature as fundamentally selfish. Bob, dressed in the latest mod fashions, noted seriously, "Yes, there is an inborn selfishness."[15] While there was agreement on this point in each of the three-generational groupings, there was no strong or total distrust of people. Only half of the immigrants felt, with Donato, "Yes, always. Once you show that you're too good, people will take advantage of you."[16] Most of the first-generation respondents agreed, but usually qualified their agreement by pointing to themselves or to a situation as Joe did, saying, "Some people don't want to be trusted. They're insecure. To some extent it's true and most definitely it's true of New York City."[17] Paul, an aspiring accountant, dissented. "If you believe this, then we would be part of a dog-eat-dog world. You must have faith in people."[18] Both the second- and third-generation respondents strongly reject the notion that people take advantage of you. As an added insight into such a feeling, there was general agreement that one could count on people. Most respondents across the three-generational span were in agreement. Maria dissented, declaring, "Today everyone is out for himself for his own benefit. The perfect example is the great corruption

12. Interview, Alfredo.
13. Interview, Lou.
14. Interview, Vincent.
15. Interview, Bob.
16. Interview, Donato.
17. Interview, Joe (teacher).
18. Interview, Paul.

in American society which is in moral decay. In this situation you can't tell who your friends are."[19] Lou, a second-generation respondent, was another dissenter who contended, "You can count on your family. In fact, primarily on your family, but outside of it you can't."[20]

Thus, there is no significant increase in the feelings of personal normlessness across a three-generational span. My findings regarding Italian immigrants are in conflict with those of Almond and Verba, in that I do not find strong evidence of personal mistrust. This may be owing to changes in Italian society since they conducted their survey. It appears that the decrease comes from the impact of the American political system in neutralizing such feelings.

When we consider perceived political normlessness, there is general agreement in a belief that other people or groups have power to the extent of ignoring the majority.[21] Most of the immigrants agreed that some groups in particular have too much power, and offered as examples businessmen, bureaucracy, the rich, and politicians.[22] It is interesting to note that the general groupings listed by the immigrants did not vary from those believed to be too powerful in Italy and the United States. As Alfredo put it, "The majority want the war to stop (Vietnam), big men oppose it. They have their investments. They can't back down."[23] There is little variation among the first-, second-, and third-generation respondents, who usually listed such specific interest groups as unions, the military, and specific industries as being too powerful. To Lou the matter was simple: "Those

---

19. Interview, Maria (housewife).
20. Some people say that most people can't be trusted and that if you don't watch out they will take advantage of you.
Interview, Lou.
21. Six questions were used as an index of political normlessness.
Question #89. One sometimes hears that some people have so much government over the way government is run that the majority are ignored. Agree? Are there any groups or individuals you believe have too much power?
22. Interview, Alfredo.
23. Interview, Lou.

who have money have power! Which then leads to the disregard of [the] majority."[24] It is significant that in the listing of power groups no religious, ethnic, or racial groups were cited by any of the respondents.

There was an overwhelming uniformity among the respondents on the issue of being given equal treatment by public officials.[25] There was agreement that they would be given equal treatment by a government official. By the nature of the responses they seemed to indicate an equality of direct access to government officials, but whether the officials would be thought willing to listen to the respondent was another matter. Most distinguish between the formal act of listening and that of acting upon the respondent's case. Gianfranco, quiet and scholarly, at present a bank clerk, said forcefully, "He may listen in that your words will be heard, but it's doubtful if your ideas penetrated. Once he gets your vote he'll turn around and forget you."[26] Mario, a young lawyer, felt similarly: "Only if you show that you could bring to bear political pressure on him. If you represent a group and have support, he can see the political repercussions.[27] This reasoning was characteristic of the second- and third-generation respondents, such as Laura, who summarized the view succinctly with "I'd be one person with no power. It's not likely he would listen."[28]

There was also strong agreement of all groups regarding the actions of political candidates.[29] Nearly all of them felt that a candidate's speeches were not binding and could not be taken at face value, since once he was elected there was

24. Interview, Lou.

25. Question #111. If you were to talk to a politician about an issue, do you think you would be given equal treatment? If you had a chance to talk to a government official would he listen to you? See Almond and Verba, pp. 74–75, 77.

26. Interview, Gianfranco.

27. Interview, Mario.

28. Interview, Laura.

29. Question #117. All candidates sound good in their speeches but you can never tell what they will do after they are elected. Agree? See: Almond and Verba, pp. 109–10.

no telling what he might do. As Gaetano said, "Once in office he'll do what he wants. He says things just to be elected."[30] Gianfranco was in agreement: "They promise what they can't deliver; they get votes and that's that."[31] Paul, a first-generation respondent, cited examples: "The perfect example was Johnson on Vietnam. Look how he changed after the election. Often it's political rhetoric or outright lying."[32] Bob tried to explain the reason for this: "He can't stick to his promises because he's made too many deals. He's got too many debts to pay off."[33] Mario dissented: "You can tell by his background. His past views and what he has done."[34] Father Andrew agreed with this view, asserting, "You must separate the rhetoric from the actual person."[35]

The final dimension of political normlessness dealt with the respondents' perceptions of where the unrest in the United States was leading.[36] There was some uncertainty expressed by the immigrants and first-generation respondents as to their future. There was uneasiness regarding their economic advancement. The second- and third-generation respondents cited general lawlessness, moral decay, and governmental indifference to people. In this dimension, they seemed to give more evidence of perceived norm deviations and felt that its continuance would endanger the survival of this society.

These data do not substantiate the Horton and Thompson position that there is a clear relationship between social mistrust and political alienation. Half of the immigrant cases indicated that they were politically normless, but the finding is not conclusive enough. There is a decided absence of perceived normlessness among the first-generation re-

30. Interview, Gaetano.
31. Interview, Gianfranco.
32. Interview, Paul.
33. Interview, Bob.
34. Interview, Mario.
35. Interview, Father Andrew.
36. Where is all this turmoil in the U. S. leading?

spondents. There is more definite evidence of political normlessness among those of the second- and, particularly, the third-generation respondents.

Family, School, and Church

A number of studies have attempted to explain the many relationships between childhood experiences and adult attitudes, and behavior patterns. They have given us needed insights into the sources of political attitudes.[37] Some studies have shown that childhood socialization practices have considerable effect on adult political attitudes and behavior.[38] Three of the most influential environments are the family, school, and church. The following pages will attempt to investigate the relationship between political alienation and the respondents' evaluation of their roles in these three environments.

At the outset, we should consider the relationship between family life and political alienation. The role of the family in southern Italian society has been considered in an earlier chapter. I took issue with Banfield's explanation that ethos was a cause of amoral familism and said, rather, that the patterns of the social structure better explain it. As Barzini has noted,

> Anarchy in Italy is not simply a way of life, a spontaneous condition of society, a natural development: it is also the deliberate product of man's will. . . . [I]t has been assiduously cultivated and strengthened down the centuries. The strength of the family is not only, therefore, the bulwark against disorder, but, at the same time, one of its principal causes. . . . The family was also invincible because it was the sacred ark in which Italians deposit and preserved against alien influences.[39]

The family is part of the political socialization process.

---

37. Adorno, *The Authoritarian Personality.*
38. Hyman, *Political Socialization;* Campbell *et al., The Voter Decides.*
39. Barzini, *The Italians,* pp. 191, 192.

It seems reasonable to conclude that the southern Italian family does not provide its offspring with a coherent view of the national political system. The earlier discussion concerning family decision-making indicates that southern Italian family experiences prepare adults to accept and to support authoritarian, rather than democratic, political structures. Decisions are rarely made on a democratic basis. There is little training in the form of the pragmatic give and take that a democratic system requires.

I have previously noted the roles of the children, the father, and the mother. One of Paulsen's respondents' description of the family affirms my conclusion.

> Papa's reasoning was this: "I am the highest authority over my family. Every decision must be evaluated by me. Each private and public act of my children is subject to my judgement."[40]

We have also previously seen that the Italian family undergoes change when it comes to a new environment. Even in the first generation there is a lessening of the role of the father in decision-making and an increase in the role of the children. The second generation shows some significant alteration in the roles of its members, particularly in the role of the mother, and in the increased discussion in the realm of decision-making. By the third generation, the Italian family becomes more democratic and modern. There is more of a shared decision-making situation, with greater room for disagreement. These findings lead us to conclude that there is a strong correlation between the decision-making process in the family and political alienation. As one moves from a constricted decision-making process among the Italian immigrants to a more open arrangement, we can see the relative decline of a sense of political powerlessness. We may conclude that those respondents who remember themselves as having little influence in family decisions are more likely to feel politically powerless than those

---

40. Paulsen, *The Searchers*, p. 241.

who recall having had a good deal of family influence. This conclusion seems to hold, regardless of occupation or sex. These findings also suggest that those who believed that the decisions in their family were subject to their influence were less likely to feel politically powerless when they reach adulthood.

The school is another significant agency of political socialization for the child. The school environment has an effect on the political orientations of individuals.[41] Almond and Verba seem to feel that the individual's experiences with authority patterns in the school environment may be generalized by the individual to the political world. They emphasize that nonpolitical experience in the family and the school are only two of many forms of political socialization and that other political experiences may actually have greater influence on political orientations in later life.[42]

From the responses of the immigrant group, we were able to construct a portrait of the Italian educational system. Rigid discipline characterizes the Italian schools. Students are exposed to a teacher-pupil relationship in which the former is the accepted and unquestioned authority. Discipline is harsh. The gap between teacher and pupil increases with the educational level. There is little room for discussion. The teacher is the counterpart of the father at all levels, in whom authority and wisdom are supposed to reside. The Italian school system tends to develop the southern Italian along the lines of the traditional social and cultural systems, thereby reinforcing the nuclear family. It does not serve as a reinforcing institution for the understanding and the development of a coherent view of the political system. Thus, the individual is ill prepared to take his place in the political system.

Almond and Verba found a distinct relationship between

---

41. Martin Levin, "Social Climates and Political Socialization," *POQ* (1961), pp. 596–606. See also Edgar Litt, "Civic Education, Community Norms, and Political Indoctrination," *ASR* 28 (1963).

42. Almond and Verba, pp. 323–28.

nonparticipation in family and school activities and low subjective political competence.[43] They found that the strength of this relationship varies among different educational groups, being strongest among the least well educated. The family and the school, for the lower levels of educated people, were practically the only sources of participant norms and other motivations that might contribute to subjective political competence. For the more highly educated individuals, a wider range of factors, such as more political information, higher social position, and higher occupational and class norms, might substitute for family and school experience in contributing to feelings of political efficacy.[44]

Experience with authority figures in nonpolitical social spheres may set up certain propensities in the individual that affect his later orientation toward political authority. Feelings of inefficacy in school and home life may contribute to low subjective political competence.

Feelings of low political efficacy may contribute to frustration and aggression, which expand into alienation from the political system.[45]

Attitudes toward the Economic Situation and Political Alienation

The traditional Marxian view of alienation sees it as growing out of the work situation in large-scale industrial capitalist enterprises. Alienation in Marxian terms was the divorce of the worker from the product of his labor. This alienation of man from his work was one of the great tragedies of industrialism.

Fromm and others see alienation and apathy as characteristic of modern industrial societies.[46] They see alienation

---

43. *Ibid.*, p. 368.
44. *Ibid.*
45. Franz Neumann, p. 290.
46. Erich Fromm, *The Scene Society;* Robert Blauner, *Alienation and Freedom.*

from work resulting in alienation in other spheres of life. Some have found that the less a man has control over his work situation, the more likely he is to be socially alienated and politically radical. We have already found that those in manual working positions are more likely to be alienated than those in nonmanual occupations. This may be because manual workers have a lower degree of control over their work situations than nonmanual workers.

The present study did not include decision-making on the job, but did consider different aspects of the economic situation. Actual occupations of the respondent were compared with his earlier ambitions and those of his parents. Among these, there seemed to be no major conflict with their parents over his occupational goals. Parents may have had certain goals in mind but the fact that their children did not achieve them was no major source of family discord. At the least, most of the respondents and their parents wanted an education. Where this goal is particularly not realized is among the immigrant respondents, where, as previously reported, the educational level tended to range from primary to secondary, usually toward the lower educational levels. There is also a difference among actual positions, early goals, and parental goals among the first-generation respondents. The discrepancy seems to lessen significantly in the second generation and in the third. There seems to be a correlation, then, with the previous findings regarding political powerlessness, in that the greatest discrepancy between current occupational position and past and recent aspirations is most pronounced among the immigrant and first-generation respondents, where political powerlessness is the highest.

Where the occupational positions of the respondents were the same as their fathers' or lower, there were significant expressions of political powerlessness. This was most pronounced among the immigrant respondents. As a result, the immigrants felt that they were not much better off than their parents, and they were not satisfied with their economic position. While first-generation respondents felt that they were better off than their parents, most were dissatisfied with their current economic situation. The picture of occupational mobility changes among the second- and third-generation Italian-Americans, who felt that their economic situation was better than that of their parents, and they were essentially satisfied with their economic situation. Thus political powerlessness, when correlated with these dimensions of the economic situation, indicates somewhat of a decline among the second-, and particularly the third-generation respondents, where the economic situation is regarded as more favorable.

Religious Bases of Political Alienation

The values of the family and the school are reinforced by the church. Hence, we must look at the church as a socializing institution. Several questions regarding church attendance were asked and later trichotomized to the categories of marginal, moderate, and strict Catholics.[47] The immigrant respondents, with only two exceptions, ranged from moderate to strict Catholic. The first- and second-generation respondents lined up similarly, ranging from moderate to strict Catholic with few exceptions. There is a significant change among those of the third generation,

---

47. I used the following questions to arrive at the strict, moderate, and marginal categories.

Question #17. Please note the phrases listed on this concerning your religion. Which one would you select to describe yourself?
a. I don't believe in any religion.
b. I am not a Catholic, but a . . .
c. I am a believer, but not a churchgoer.
d. I go to Mass irregularly, but I believe.
e. I go to Mass regularly.
f. I receive Communion at least two or three times a year.
g. I receive Communion at least once a month.
Options c. and d. define a marginal Catholic, e. a moderate, f. and g. a strict Catholic. See Lawrence E. Hazelrigg, "Religious and Class Bases of Political Conflict"; p.   . Abbott, pp. 101-3.

who were generally marginal Catholics. Most of the immigrants look at religion as a guide or a foundation for a
person's life. Some expressed it in terms of having to believe
in something. Joe, a teacher and first-generation respondent,
looked upon it as "a restraint to individual behavior. It
stops poor or unsocial behavior."[48] The first generation
deviated little as to the role religion plays in their lives.
Mario deviated sharply, declaring, "Religion is important
in everyday life in Italy, but not in the United States. Here
you go to a lawyer for help, in Italy you go to the Church.
In my life it's not important for I totally reject the notion
of God."[49] Most second- and third-generation respondents
looked upon religion as a guide in life, although Sal lamented, "Before it was more of a guide. It kept you honest.
Now it's more of business. It's changed and so have its teach-
ings. I will adhere to the old rules of the Church; the new
ones are not worth anything."[50]

Among the immigrants there is less evidence of change
in their practices from their earlier years, while most of
the first, second, and third generation asserted that they
have become less religious than when they were younger.[51]
Paul said: "I was brought up very religiously. I became dis-
enchanted with the structure. The priests don't practice
what they teach. I've felt cheated and disappointed."[52] Maria
explained it this way, "When I was younger I just accepted
it . . . now I think more about it and question."[53] The latter seems to be typical of the second generation. Most of
the immigrants, first-, and third-generation respondents said
that they differed significantly from the practices and beliefs of their parents in their being less strict about their
religion. The second-generation respondents on the whole

48. Interview, Joe.
49. Interview, Mario.
50. Interview, Sal.
51. Russo, title.
52. Interview, Paul.
53. Interview, Maria.

seemed to feel that they did not differ much from their parents.[54]

Marginal Catholics tended to be more uniformly and unequivocally in favor of the changes made by the Vatican Council and urged more to follow. Strict Catholics were against such changes and decried what they termed to be the ruin of the Church. Moderate Catholics tended to be receptive, but qualified their approval in various ways.

Almost unanimously, the respondents did not feel that the Church should speak its mind on politics, and called for the separation of Church and state. This did not vary along generational lines, nor according to the marginal to strict Catholic dimension. But there was some ambiguity on this point. When the question was posed: Should the Church speak out on social issues, such as poverty, and so on, there was a great deal of contradiction. We might consider the responses of Father Tomaso, an immigrant priest, and Father Andrew, a third-generation respondent. Father Tomaso asserted that "one couldn't separate political man and spiritual man into two distinct spheres. Very often there is conflict between the two spheres." This view leads to a position of involvement in politics. Father Andrew, on the other hand, asserted the importance of the Church-and-state separation. The Church should influence, but not participate in, the political process. He contended that it should express its opinions on social issues and even publicize them. Even with Father Andrew there is some contradiction, in that he participates in a number of organizations that are political or are agencies of the government. He also was a supporter of a local candidate and worked on his behalf. This ambiguity, then, is not confined to just those outside of the clergy. Gaetano, an unskilled worker in a local dye house, felt that "they are separate areas, but

54. Bernard Lazerwitz and Louis Rowitz, "The Three Generation Hypothesis," *AJS* 69 (March 1964) : 529–38. See also Francis X. Femminella, "The Impact of Italian Migration and American Catholicism," *The American Catholic Sociological Review* 22 (Fall 1961) : 233–41.

if there are not enough honest people in politics to speak
the truth, then the church must do it. Particularly, the
Church must act to combat Communist propaganda, since
the people have no one to battle against it and speak the
truth."[55] Donato admitted almost scornfully, "They should
speak out on these kinds of issues, but not in the pulpit.
Perhaps by meetings with other priests or bishops, but they
shouldn't meddle in politics."[56] Paul reaffirmed his position,
"They must speak out but shouldn't press government by
political activity in any particular direction. Speaking out
does not mean involvement."[57] The discrepancy between
assertions of separation of church and state on the one hand
and speaking out on issues that may lead to political action
on the other is more apparent among the third-generation
respondents. Vincent, an aspiring law student, who had
previously held to the separation-of-Church-and-State doc-
trine was typical of them when he now said, "It should
speak out on the social issues and get involved in changing
these conditions. There is too much money placed in buildings while people are starving."[58] Father Andrew had been
saying the same thing, but in essence he was doing the
opposite by an actual political involvement.

In conclusion, it appears that the strict-Catholic category
tends to be associated with low political alienation. The
moderate-Catholic category is associated with low political
normlessness but a higher sense of political powerlessness.
The marginal-Catholic category is associated with a higher
sense of political normlessness and a relative decline in political powerlessness.

Conclusion

We have found that a number of stimuli from various

55. Interview, Gaetano.
56. Interview, Donato.
57. Interview, Paul.
58. Interview, Vincent.

sources in Italian society are rooted in the Italian past to produce an isolating and fragmented political culture. I have referred to this society as one of inner antagonism.

Though powerlessness is strongest through the second generation and declines significantly in the third generation, it still persists.

I have suggested that Italian women would feel more politically powerless, while Italian men would more likely perceive norm violations. The politically alienated among the Italian immigrants are in the 18–30-year-old age bracket, while the Italian-Americans fall into the 31–50 age category. The average age of the politically alienated was 30.6. The lower mobility rates accounted for the alienation of Italian-Americans in this age category. Lower levels of education among the immigrants and first-, and second-generation respondents is positively correlated with high political powerlessness.

The movement from a small rural environment to a large city brings with it the sense of loss of control of that environment. The persistence of political powerlessness into the third generation is owing to a structural separation. A low position in the social structure is interpreted as the inability to acquire the means to achieve desired ends. We have previously found that our respondents do not place high in the income, occupational, and residential categories. Alienation among manual workers seems to reflect the lack of control of their work environment. In part this results from lack of occupational preparation for urban living among Italian immigrants, which persists strongly into the first generation.[59] Our findings suggest that there has not been massive group advancement into the higher income, occupational, and residential categories, owing in part to a structural separation, which serves to perpetuate feelings of powerlessness through the third generation.[60]

---

59. Danilo Dolci, *Report from Palermo* (New York: Orion Press, 1956).
60. I will discuss the particular responses of the alienated in chapter 7.

7

Political Alienation and Political Participation among Italian-Americans

In this section we will explore the relationship between political alienation and political participation, considering the attitudinal and behavioral variables of political alienation.

The politically alienated among Italian immigrants and Italian-Americans are not organization joiners; they incline to little political activity. Strong party identifiers in both the immigrant and Italian-American groupings are less likely to be alienated. Political alienation does not appear to affect voter turnout nor does it lead to a further decrease in political interest. This is because of appeals to the alienated based on their need for political power, and appeals based on the need of both immigrants and the Italian-Americans for ethnic recognition. Political powerlessness and perceived political normlessness among both groups may interact in a populist candidate. What may stir the immigrants and Italian-Americans into political action is a defense of acculturated values, which they perceive as being threatened.

Some studies see political apathy as one of the most common expressions of political alienation.[1] The politically alienated, they argue, see no possibility of changing anything in the system through their own efforts. Interest in politics may be viewed as both an aspect of political participation and a rough index of the degree of political apathy.[2] Participation variables in the literature have been seen as both independent and dependent variables in predicting levels of political participation. Some consider the effects of political alienation on voting behavior.[3] Almond and Verba emphasize organizational affiliations as preceding feelings of competence, while competence itself is seen as a result of the diffusion of group values to the members. Dahl has suggested that actual participation and feelings of efficacy probably reinforce each other. Subjective competence may precede participation, but the skills and familiarity with the political process that result from participation are likely, in turn, to increase the sense of ability to influence the system.[4] Agger has shown that political cynicism is related to frequency of political discussion.[5]

1. Franz Neuman, *The Democratic and the Authoritarian State*, p. 290.

2. Several studies have found a positive correlation between interest in and knowledge about politics. See Campbell, *The American Voter*.

3. Horton and Thompson, "Political Alienation as a Force in Political Action." See also Kenneth Janda, "A Comparative Study of Political Alienation and Voting in Three Suburban Communities," in *Studies in History and Social Science* (Normal, Ill.: Illinois State University Press, 1965), pp. 53–68; Aberbach, "Alienation and Political Behavior", pp. 93–98.

4. Dahl, *Who Governs?*, p. 26.

5. *Discussion*

Question #94. Have you talked politics with anyone recently? What was the nature of your discussion?

Question #95. Do you ever discuss politics with friends or relatives?

Question #97. Is there anyone today whose opinions on politics you particularly admire?

Ideology

Question #87. In general are you interested in politics? Have you ever been interested in the politics of Italy?

Organization

Question #117. Do you pay much attention to campaigning? Is it needed or would we be better off without it?

At the outset we will explore the relationship of political interest and political alienation. I have selected six questions that will serve as an index of political interest. Talking about politics is the most common form of political activity.[6] I found that most of the politically alienated among the Italian immigrants had talked "politics" with someone a short time before the period in which they were interviewed. The excitement generated by a local candidate, an Italian by nationality, seemed to be a major factor in increasing the discussion level among some of the respondents. There was no variation on this finding along the three-generational span. However, whether this was a regular occurrence is another matter. We tend to think that among the politically alienated among all groups, the frequency of political discussion is not high. Most, in fact, tended not to discuss politics among friends and relatives.

Most of the politically alienated among the immigrant respondents tended not to follow accounts of politics in the newspapers or the other media on a regular basis. One of the influencing factors is not only a certain cultural outlook[7] toward things political, but also a lack of facility with the language. Also, their alien status and their inability to vote seems to influence their interest and political participation levels in America.[8] However, the American political system serves to increase the interest among the Italians, as evidenced by the higher rates of those who follow political

Question #120. Can you think of any election in which you were particularly interested?

6. See Dwaine Marvick and Charles Nixon, "Recruitment Contrasts in Rival Campaign Groups," in Dwaine Marvick, ed., *Political Decision Makers* (Glencoe, Ill.: The Free Press, 1961), pp. 193–217; Stein Rokkan and Angus Campbell, "Norway and the U. S. of America," *International Science Journal* 12 (1960): 69–99. Their studies indicate that persons participating in informal political discussions are more likely than nondiscussants to vote and participate in the political process. See also Patrick J. Gallo, "Ethnicity and Socio-Political Preferences: The Jews of New York City," *Rassegna Italiana di Sociologia* (April–June 1973).

7. Barzini, *The Italians*. See also Almond and Verba, p. 308.

8. W. S. Robinson, "The Motivational Structure of Political Participation," *ASR* 19 (1952): 151–56.

accounts among the first-generation respondents. This pattern continues, however, more strongly among the second- and third-generation respondents.

The politically alienated among the immigrants were not able to point to an election either in Italy or the United States that aroused their interest. Again the picture changes among the first-, second-, and third-generation respondents. Most in these three groups cited the Presidential campaign of 1968 and the New York mayoralty campaign of 1969. Interest in the latter may be partially explained by the fact that there were two candidates of Italian extraction. The latter election generated interest as a result of Nixon's appeals to the apathetic among the electorate.

When we looked at another dimension of interest, namely, those who are involved in political campaigns, we found that the politically alienated among the immigrants paid attention to campaigns, but did not follow them closely.[9] There was no significant increase in the interest level in this respect along the three-generational span, although there was a slight relative increase. This is explained by some of the previous findings that political interest, particularly among Italians, is highest around election time, but declines significantly afterwards. Among the immigrants, the interest and political involvement seem to center around the campaign, which they view as spectators, and is focused on the act of voting. As we shall see later, the presence of an ethnic candidate may serve to stimulate political activity beyond just voting.

Most of the immigrants, when drawn to the political arena, were not able to cite anyone whose political opinions they admired, although the pattern is reversed among those of the first-, and especially the second- and third-generation Italians. It is also significant to note that the epople whose opinions they admired generally agreed with their own

9. Campbell, *The American Voter*, pp. 27–115. See also Lane, *Political Life*, pp. 161, 440.

ideological orientations. My findings of a relative increase in the interest level among the first-, second-, and third-generation respondents as contrasted to the immigrants runs contrary to those found elsewhere. Others have found a correlation between a low level of political interest, political apathy, and political participation.[10] The fact that I was not able to detect a major difference among the politically alienated and nonalienated may be accounted for in a variety of ways. First, the size of the sample may have inhibited reaching a more meaningful conclusion. Second, my interviews took place prior to election, and the relative increase in interest level, which I conclude occurs among all Italian respondents, may have been reflected in my findings. However, I have merely determined that the low interest level among the politically alienated Italian immigrants may be neutralized by the American political system, in that political interest along the three-generational span seems to increase independently of alienation. We may have to look elsewhere for the explanation. We should also note at this point that I have not determined the quality of that interest.[11]

Another indicator of political participation is organizational membership. Most of the respondents across the three-generational span were not joiners of organizations. The organization that the respondents belonged to most frequently was a union, or some other economic or professional associations related to their occupation.[12] The immigrants tended to belong either to a local social center of other immigrants, or to clubs made up of fellow towns-

10. Abbott, "Political Alienation in Mexico and Italy," p. 168. See also Campbell, *The American Voter*, pp. 103–5. While these authors show correlations between nonparticipation and low interest by the inefficacious, there is no evidence that they are protest voters in national elections.

11. Campbell, *The American Voter*.

12. Some studies have found that Labor union members are more likely to take an interest in politics, to have stronger stands on issues, and to vote than are nonunion laboring persons. William R. McPhee and William Glaser, eds., *Public Opinion and Congressional Elections* (Glencoe, Ill.: The Free Press, 1962).

men from Italy.[13] Only three respondents out of the entire group would be considered high organizational joiners. High organization membership then would tend to be associated with reduced feelings of political powerlessness. However, membership in general voluntary organizations alone, without participation in the political process itself, does not seem substantially to reduce feelings of political powerlessness. High organizational membership has no effect in reducing political normlessness.

Political alienation does not seem to have a great effect on the level of voter turnout among our respondents.[14] I reported earlier that regularity of voting is characteristic of the respondents of all groups. The immigrants are more prone not to report their party vote; this is not the case among the other groupings.

In order to assess the nature of political activity, I constructed an index ranging from the lower to the higher forms.[15] The Italian immigrants who were politically alienated were at the lower end of the continuum of political activity. This held true of their political activity in Italy and the United States.

As one moves from the first generation to the third generation of Italian-American respondents, there is a gradual increase in political activity. This increase, I hasten to add, seemed to occur at election time and fell off significantly afterward. In other words, the particular election may have stirred the respondents to political action, but it did not have a lasting effect. In addition, the presence of one or

---

13. Almond and Verba, pp. 246–64.
14. Abbott, p. 131.
15. *Organizations*
    Question #128. Have you ever done any of the following?
    a. spoken to someone in office on an issue?
    b. written a letter on an issue to someone in political office.
    c. gone to a political rally.
    d. asked people to vote for one candidate over another.
    e. worked for a political candidate.
    f. led or took part in a protest demonstration.
    g. taken part in a strike.

more Italian-Amerian candidates seemed to be a major determinant.

The mayoralty campaign of 1969, which had two Italian-Americans running for office, Mario Procaccino and John Marchi, was cited as an example in which the respondents were both interested and active. The other was the primary campaign of an Italian-American, which had a similar effect. Ethnicity was in both instances the most significant determinant in increased level of political interest and political activity. The same people whose interest and activity increased in the mayoralty campaign of 1969, and who favored the conservative candidates, now supported a liberal candidate in 1970. In the former instance, the Italian-American respondents were not acting in a negative sense. Rather, it was for the defense of such acculturated values as individual initiative, security, and the like. The politically alienated among the Italian-Americans sensed the fulfillment of their need for political power. In the congressional primary of an Italo-American candidate, we see the same two factors at work. The particular district from which he was running was heavily Italian-American, yet it had not fielded a successful Italian-American candidate for years. Hence the presence of an Italian-American candidate served to fill two needs: recognition and political power.

In both campaigns there was an increase in political activity among the respondents, particularly as one moved from the first- to the third-generational groupings. In particular, there was an involvement in the form of attending political rallies and working for the candidates. In the congressional campaign a number of the first- and second- generation respondents were actively involved in the petition-signing process.

The involvement of many of the respondents in these two instances did not seem to have a lasting effect. There is no indication that these same respondents continued at the same level of political activity after the elections. To some extent this may be explained by the fact that in both cases their candidates were unsuccessful. For those Italian-Americans who were politically alienated, the 1969 mayoralty campaign and the 1970 congressional primary campaign temporarily neutralized their alienated feelings, but in the long run they may have sharpened them, due to the failure of these Italian-American candidates to win public office. The primary victory of Frank Rizzo in Philadelphia also illustrates the relationship between ethnicity and increased political activity among Italian-Americans. His candidacy resulted in a 105% increase over 1970 among Italian-American voters. This was a greater increase than any other voting group in Philadelphia exhibited. Mr. Rizzo carried all seven Italian wards by a margin of nearly 30,000 over his nearest opponent. Ethnic identification alone cannot account for his overwhelming victory. Rizzo won six Irish and five Wasp wards by margins of 4 to 1. He also cut sharply into the Jewish vote by capturing almost 50% of the vote.[16]

Some studies have indicated that party identification is established early in life and remains quite stable over the lifetime of most individuals. Since party identification has a great impact on attitudes of individuals, it seems reasonable to suggest that party identification might have some effect on the likelihood of an individual becoming alienated. Party identification might affect system acceptance. While this may have some validity in explaining the political alienation of some of our native respondents, it does not hold for our immigrant respondents. Some studies have indicated that most party identifiers have inherited their party identification from their families.[17] Few go out and choose a party, although this is what happened in Italy following World War II. It was at this time that many new parties were

16. "The Philadelphia Story," *Politéia* 1 (Autumn 1971) : 12–13.
17. Campbell, p. 147. See also David Easton and Jack Dennis, "The Child's Image of Government," *The Annals of the American Academy of Political and Social Sciences* (September 1965) , pp. 40–57. Fred I. Greenstein, *Children and Politics* (New Haven: Yale University Press, 1965) .

formed. Here was a situation in which alienation or non-alienation preceded party identification, indicating that among the immigrants political alienation probably affected party preference. It would seem, then, that party identifiers would be more likely than nonidentifiers to participate in politics, to have high levels of political information, to be politically interested and to be familiar with their political history.[18]

I found that the politically alienated among the immigrants have a low-to-moderate ability to identify important personalities connected with Italian politics both past and present. Similarly, there was a low-to-moderate ability to name the principal parties in Italy. There was a decidedly low ability to understand important issues in the United States and a low-to-moderate ability to identify key public officials. Most were able to list what they considered to be the principal problems in the United States and Italy. In the former case, most listed the Vietnam war and race. In the latter case, most felt that it was unemployment or underemployment, and a general condition of political chaos. There was a decided improvement in terms of understanding the nature of the principal issues facing the United States among the first-, second-, and third-generation respondents. Most in all three groups listed the war and either race or a social issue as principal problems facing the United States. There was a rather high ability to identify high governmental leaders among the first- and second-generation respondents.

Party identification may serve as an interpretive device for the citizen and a screen for political perceptions.[19] Allegiance to parties associated with the constitutional status quo may influence identifiers toward positive attitudes about the system. One with no such identification would have no such reinforcement. One who identified with a party that

18. Abbott, p. 131.
19. Campbell, pp. 387-93. See also Abbott, pp. 146-52.

rejects the political regime might be influenced to reject the political system by his identification with such a party. Party identification seems to be associated with levels of political alienation. Party identification in itself does not seem to have any independent relationship to low political alienation. Political alienates among the Italian immigrants are less likely than nonalienates to have voted for the status-quo parties while they were in Italy, and are more likely to have voted for anti-system parties. This pattern seems to hold true, however, only for party identifiers. Alienates who have not identified with a party seem to lack the sophistication to select a party that would express their feelings of dissatisfaction. Thus, they have no point of reference on which to base their decision.

Recent studies have pointed out the importance and influence that party identification has on many aspects of political behavior and attitudes.[20] While the major political parties in America may not be viewed as anti-system parties, perhaps individual party candidates may be so perceived. Mr. Procaccino may have been cast in the latter role. His constant references to the "limousine liberals" and "the subway people" made it a contest between the average man and the people with doormen. In a sense Mr. Procaccino campaigned as an urban populist, and in his campaign he placed the blame for society's problems on Wall Street and the Eastern Establishment. As he told one of his audiences,

> City College is what New York is all about. City College has always had more heart than Harvard. It has always been more real than Yale. And it has always had more purpose than Princeton. . . . It was built on the sacrifices by our mothers and fathers and ourselves. The sacrifices of our mothers who walked blocks to save a few cents for groceries.[21]

---

20. Angus Campbell et al., *The Voter Decides* (Evanston, Ill.: Row, Peterson & Co., 1954) . See also Campbell, *The American Voter*, pp. 12, 167; Bernard Berelson, "Communication and Public Opinion," in Wilbur Schramm, ed., *Mass Communications* (Urbana, Ill.: University of Illinois Press, 1949) , pp. 496–512.
21. *New York Times*, August 31, 1969.

John Lindsay was a candidate of the liberal and independent parties. He was also a graduate of Yale and a member of the university's governing board. Powerlessness and political normlessness may have interacted significantly in the New York mayoralty election. This may be borne out by the voting preferences revealed by the respondents. First- and second-generation respondents favored Procaccino, while most of those of the third generation preferred Mayor Lindsay. Ethnicity was a major determinant in these preferences, a stronger causal factor in this instance than feelings of alienation.[22]

Horton and Thompson have not only found an expected relationship between powerlessness and negative voting, but they present some evidence that powerlessness by itself has an independent effect on voting behavior.[23] On local issues, a perceived sense of powerlessness does not seem to lead to negative voting or to opposition to certain controversial programs. However, it is not clear just what effect distrust of local government exerts or how it interacts with feelings of powerlessness.

Templeton on national issues found alienation unrelated to respondents' party identification or voting behavior in 1956 and 1960.[24] Levin and Eden find some support for the assertion that the quality of the vote cast by an alienated may be different from that of the nonalienated in that it tends to be negative. Since both parties present themselves "as responsible national voices and both are in fact committed to the established political system . . . neither provides the citizen with the opportunity to validate his personal rejection of the political system."[25] As a result the politically alienated will tend to withdraw from political activity manifesting his inconsistent voting by vacillating

22. I shall have more to say about this in the following chapter.
23. Horton and Thompson, p. 425.
24. Templeton, pp. 252–55.
25. Ibid., p. 256.

between major parties, low political knowledge and interest particularly on a national level.[26]

My findings seem to indicate that people of low socio-economic status, as determined by education, income, and occupation, have objectively less power in the community than do higher-status individuals and therefore naturally feel more powerless and more alienated.[27] Thus, it is not an individual's merely subjective belief that he is incapable of achieving any modification of his position through political action that leads to alienation; rather it is his true, objective lack of power.

The politically alienated among the Italians do not express their condition by withdrawing completely from political activity. They can be mobilized for political action by either appeals on ethnic lines or by appeals fulfilling their need for political power. Data gathered in this study suggested that ethnic voting is likely to be the strongest among lower-middle-class Italians. Membership in the ethnic group is important not only in its own right but also as a means of obtaining substantial benefits. Ethnic voting among middle-class Italian-Americans will tend to be at a lower level than that of the lower-middle class. A vote on strict ethnic lines will occur when the Italian candidate agrees to protect their newly acquired position, for they are seeking to consolidate their new status. A significant drop in ethnic voting will be evident among upper-middle-class Italian-Americans, who are in a position to put aside those issues of substance and material rewards which affect the people of the lower middle class and those status-laden issues which are most important to middle-class Italian-Americans. The more highly educated, upper-income Italians across the three-generational span seem to vote Republican in national

---

26. Persons who feel efficacious politically are much more likely to become actively involved in politics. Almond and Verba, *The Civic Culture;* Campbell, *The American Voter;* Dahl, *Who Governs?*

27. Horton and Thompson, pp. 190–95.

elections. Those of a low SES tend to vote Democratic in national elections. The middle-income Italian-American[28] in national elections tends to identify with the Democrats in times of severe economic stress, while in periods of prosperity they tend to identify with the Republicans.[29] The upper-income Italian-American respondents in 1968 voted for Nixon, while those of lower socioeconomic status favored Humphrey. The middle-income Italian-Americans tended to favor Nixon in 1968, thus identifying with the upper-SES Italian-Americans.[30]

My earlier discussion of religion and class would lead to the conclusion that Italians of the same social class-ethni-class, and a lower one at that, will have less economic security and thus feel that they have less control over their political environment.[31] The threat of deprivation to upper-strata Italians that is present in the politics of the welfare state may provide greater motivation for political participation than the promise of reward to the lower-SES Italians. The relation of an issue to the Italians' interest as an ethnic group tends to be more visible among upper-strata Italians. Upper-strata Italians are more inclined toward political participation, since they can influence policy and reap the rewards more readily than lower-strata Italians, who can in-

28. Bernard Berelson *et al.*, *Voting* (Chicago: University of Chicago Press, 1954). Heinz Eulau, *Class and Party in the Eisenhower Years* (New York: The Free Press, 1962). The authors point out that middle-class persons are exposed to more stimuli about politics than working-class people. Several other studies have shown that upper SES persons, especially the better educated, are more likely to develop efficacious feelings. See Campbell, *The American Voter;* Dahl, *Who Governs?*

29. Upwardly mobile persons may become active in politics as part of their effort to move upward. Dwaine Marvick and Charles Nixon, "Recruitment Contrasts in Rival Campaign Groups," in Marvick, ed., *Political Decision-Makers* (Glencoe, Ill.: The Free Press, 1961), pp. 193–217; Mattei Dogan, "Political Ascent in a Class Society: French Deputies 1870–1958," in idem.

30. We have seen earlier that religion tends to be a major determinant in the ideological orientation of Italians in local politics. On the national level, social class tends to be the determinant of party vote.

31. Lane, *Political Life*, p. 224.

fluence and benefit only by group activity and member-ship.[32] The social norms of upper-strata Italians tend to emphasize political participation. As the Italian becomes acculturated and improves his socioeconomic status he acquires the attitudes of social and civic responsibility of the Protestant ethos.[33] Lower-strata Italians are more inclined to be influenced by the cross-pressures of ethnic versus class identification.[34] They are likely to belong to fewer organizations. Lower-strata Italians are more likely to be politically alienated; a low position in the social structure is viewed by Italians as the inaccessibility to the means to achieve desired ends—social, economic, and political—and hence his exclusion from sharing in the dominant institutions, roles, and values of American society.

Conclusion

It thus appears that in the three-generational groupings the politically alienated are not organizational joiners. The most frequent form of organizational membership was in economic groups, such as unions and professional groups. While this finding is true of those who are politically powerless, it also holds for those who possess feelings of high political normlessness. High organizational membership is associated with reduced political powerlessness. Membership in general voluntary organizations without participation in the political process does not seem to reduce feelings of political powerlessness; moreover, high organizational membership has no effect in reducing political normlessness.

Political alienation does not affect the level of voter turn-

---

32. Berelson, Lazarsfeld, McPhee, pp. 156–60. See also Celia Heller, "Class as an Explanation of Ethnic Differences in Mobility Aspirations," IMR 2 (Fall 1967) : 31–39. Warner and Srole, p. 93.

33. Banfield, *The Moral Basis of a Backward Society*, p. 40. See also Heinz Eulau, "Identification With Class and Political Perspective," *Journal of Politics* 18 (1956) : 242.

34. Robert Hodge and Donald Treiman, "Class Identification in the U. S.," *AJS* 73 (March 1963) : 535–47.

out among the immigrant and Italian-American respondents. The members in both of these groupings appear to vote regularly.

While political activity is seen to increase as one moves from the first- to the third-generation Italian-Americans, much of it among the immigrants is confined to the act of voting. There is some evidence of first-, second-, and third-generation respondents inclining in the direction of involvement in campaigns when the candidate is a fellow Italian-American, and where his election would fulfill their need for political power and recognition. I hasten to add that this form of involvement is sporadic and of limited duration. In other words, when the campaign is over, or the issue that attracted their interest is removed, political activity declines significantly.

Weak party identifiers among the immigrants and Italian-Americans are less likely to be politically active and are more likely to be politically alienated.

The politically alienated among the Italian immigrants and Italian-Americans generally withdraw from political activity, particularly on a national level. But this is not their only response. Often they are stirred to political action by ethnic appeals and appeals to fulfill their need for political power.

8
Conclusions

This study has attempted to ascertain if the American political system tended toward the integration or exclusion of an ethnic group. By focusing on the Italian-American, I have sought to find out whether the American political system tended to neutralize or sharpen their sense of exclusion from the dominant values, roles, and institutions of American society.

I have also pointed out the limitations of the in-depth interview of a small number of people. I asserted that concentration on the individual runs the risk of not describing the larger societal matrix. The interview schedule has attempted to overcome this shortcoming by incorporating a number of aspects of this matrix, such as group memberships, occupational history, and the like. I have not employed the term *sample* in a strict sense. The danger of selecting a small number of people from such a large Italian-American population has been duly acknowledged. My respondents conformed closely in regional and demographic characteristics to those of the Italian-American population. I add that because this study is exploratory in nature, my findings must be stated in terms of probabilities.

The investigation has been guided by a previous model, which viewed the interaction and eventual feedback among stimuli, individual predispositions, and responses. The study has considered such stimuli as social class, religion, ethnic group membership, and structural separation. These are seen interacting with familism, a cultural predisposition that is internalized as a personal predisposition that further interacts with a set of responses. The responses were considered in chapters 5, 6, and 7.

Initially, all our Italian respondents were found to be urban residents. All of the members of the control group resided in New Jersey suburban communities. Italian immigrants come to the United States with certain expectations and anxieties. They also come with something of an urban outlook. All of our immigrant respondents had attended the cinema at least once in their lifetime. Fourteen out of fifteen of the immigrant respondents viewed television on a regular basis. Thirteen of them visited a large city at least ten times a year. My overall percentages on these three dimensions are higher than those of Polizzi.[1] The old rural culture in Italy is giving way to urbanization and industrialization. In spite of the momentum of this process, the southern Italian immigrant comes to the United States ill equipped occupationally. For a variety of reasons, the Italian subsociety becomes a source of psychological satisfaction and security. To the immigrant the active reality that is the community is the subsociety of the larger society. To the members of the control group, the concept of community is much broader. They identify with the larger society because they are members of that society. To the immigrant the Italian subsociety serves as a kind of buffer

1. J. A. Polizzi, "Southern Italian Society: Its Peasantry and Change" (Ph.D. dissertation, Cornell University, 1968).

between its members and the strangeness of a new society. It is also a launching pad from which the Italian immigrant may move toward greater interaction with the broader society. The conscious sharing of language, religion, values, and norms gives the subsociety a self-awareness and its unity. My findings with regard to the role that the subsociety plays for the Italian immigrant confirms the conclusions of Eisenstadt, Germani, and Fitzpatrick.[2] The Italian subsociety develops out of a number of interacting forces, which include previous Italian immigration patterns, the family-link type of immigration, the immigrant's psychological needs, and an out-group rejection.

Italian residential patterns remain relatively stable. The majority of my immigrant respondents were born in cities of 5,000 or less inhabitants, and resided in them prior to coming to the United States. Four out of five of the first-generation respondents were born in cities of 20,000 to 50,000 people. All of them were currently residing in cities of 100,000 or more. All of the second- and third-generation respondents were born and currently residing in cities of 100,000 or more. Thus, as one moves from the first to the third generation, the size of the city of birth and of the city of current residence increases. In contrast, the large majority of the control group were born in communities of 10,000 or less and were currently residing in communities of 20,000 or less. All of the members of the control group were residentially more mobile than the Italian respondents, as is indicated by the frequency of changed residences and their movement to different sections of the country. Moreover, the communities in which the members of the control group resided were white Protestant. As one moves across

2. S. N. Eisenstadt, The *Absorption of Immigrants* (London: Routledge & Kegan Paul Ltd., 1952) ; Gino Germani in Philip Hauser, ed., *Handbook for Social Research in Urban America* (UNESCO, 1965) ; Joseph Fitzpatrick, "The Importance of Community in the Process of Immigrant Assimilation," *IMR* (Fall 1966) .

the generational span, the total number of years of residence at the respondent's current address increased from 8.1 among those of the first generation, to 14.2 among those of the third-generation Italian-Americans. In addition, the persistence of residence in Italian-American neighborhoods is clearly evident among all generational groupings. The primary group relationships of all generational groupings are confined to other Italians of the same social class. The members of the control group confined their primary group relationships in particular to other white Protestants. There is a direct relationship among the respondents between the number of non-Italian friends and the number of formal groups joined, particularly among those of the second and third generation. I conclude that residential segregation among the Italians of all generational groupings tends to be inversely related to indicators of their socioeconomic status and assimilation, and directly related to their social distance from the core society. Italian-Americans in all generational groupings who are highly segregated tend to stand in direct proportion to those who are politically alienated.

I have held that Banfield's amoral familism still retains a core of validity.[3] I agree with Silverman[4] that ethos is not an adequate explanation of amoral familism. Amoral familism is rooted in the southern Italian social structure. I have held that familism refers to a pervasive psychic interest and cultural value that arise from the family system of southern Italy. Familism is a cultural characteristic of the southern Italian social structure, which is internalized and becomes a personal predisposition. The social system of southern Italy lacks moral sanctions outside of the family. In addition, the social system of southern Italy is disjunctive and one in which the various strata tend toward closure. As a result, the southern Italian is unable to support com-

---

3. Banfield, *The Moral Basis of a Backward Society.*
4. Silverman, "Amoral Familism Reconsidered."

munity-wide interests, and community remains a weak structural unit. The southern Italian immigrant respondents bring this predisposition with them to America.

The principal variables that determine the process of the Italian immigrant's assimilation are his basic motivations and role expectations, and the demands made upon him by the broader society. The Italian immigrants seek the fulfillment of certain instrumental goals in the United States. Participation in the broader society is limited as a result of living in the subsociety, further restricting the immigrants to fewer roles. Lack of work skills and language difficulties inhibited their assumption of new roles and mark the immigrants off from the rest of society. However, there is another dimension to the limitation of roles for the Italians. The institutionalization of the Italian's behavior occurs within the social structure of the United States. An out-group rejection becomes evident in the demands and expectations made upon the Italian by the larger society.

While the Italian acculturates rapidly, there is no outright rejection of a group identity. Ten of the immigrant respondents thought of themselves as being Italian. All of the first-, and second-, and most of the third-generation respondents thought of themselves as Italian-Americans. All respondents thought that others in the broader society thought of them as Italians. The process of acculturation for the Italian is usually complete by the end of the first generation. Acculturation brings a rapid decline in interest in Italian customs. There is a quick loss of knowledge of the Italian language. Italian cooking, however, and the Italian name are major points of identity for the respondents in all generational groupings. The Italian still favors in-group marriages, although there is a predilection toward out-group marriages among the second- and third-generation respondents.

Assimilation among Italians occurs in part on these five

levels: marital, attitude receptional, behavior receptional, civil, and social assimilative. The Italian is not identificationally or structurally assimilated. The most important level finds the Italian structurally unassimilated, as evidenced by an occupational, income, and residential differentiation from the core society. Most of the respondents held semi-skilled and unskilled positions. While mobility from the manual to nonmanual positions is relatively high in the United States, it is largely confined to skilled workers. Unskilled and semi-skilled workers have a much smaller chance of improvement than skilled workers.[5] Only two of the entire sample could be considered in the upper income brackets. Our Italian respondents view the social structure as unneutral and dominated by the core culture. The Italian perceives an out-group rejection, evidenced by the following: first, the stigma of the Italian's association with organized crime; second, a low self-image, which is initiated and substantiated by the broader society; third, their nationality, which serves as a barrier to advancement.[6]

A structural separation results in the persistence of the Italian subsociety, not its destruction as one would assume would occur with time, increased affluence, or movement to the suburbs. The residential patterns of all the respondents were remarkably stable. The greatest residential mobility occurred among the first-generation respondents. Residential stability characterizes both the second- and third-generation groupings. Movement in all three groupings tends to be to other Italian-American neighborhoods. The average length of residence in the present neighborhood of the respondents was 8.1 years for the first generation; 13 years for the second; 14.2 years for the third generation. The first- and second-generation respondents lived

5. Giuseppe Di Palma, *Apathy and Mass Participation* (Berkeley, Calif.: University of California Press, 1970).
6. Baltzell, *The Protestant Establishment.* See William Domhoff, *Who Rules America?* (Englewood Cliffs, N. J.: Prentice Hall, 1957).

in Italian-American neighborhoods, with no real mixture with other ethnic or racial groups. There was some greater evidence of mixture among the third-generation respondents, although there was still a strong representation of Italians in the neighborhood.

Whereas familism resulted in the absence of links between the family and community in southern Italy, living in the Italian subsociety leads to the development of a sense of community. Membership in the subsociety binds its members in a network of relationships that permit them to remain with it for most of their primary and some of their secondary relationships. While there was some minor evidence of mixture in the friendship patterns of the first-generation respondents, the most intimate were with fellow Italians. The same pattern remains with the second- and third-generation respondents, with an increased mixture of friends among the latter principally in the form of business associations. The most intimate friendships in all groupings were still with fellow Italians.

I have contended that the Italian subsociety is created by the intersection of the vertical stratifications of ethnicity and the horizontal stratifications of social class, which I have referred to as ethniclass. The separate units of the Italian subsociety are localized in space in communities that are linked with others by ethnicity and class. Those who were most segregated in the central city are the most concentrated in the suburbs. The Italians bring their institutions and social patterns with them in their movement to the suburbs. In spite of the loss of an ecological base, the subsociety continues to thrive. Increased affluence only serves as a means to support the subsociety's parallel social structure. In addition, ethnically related issues are transferred to the suburbs.

The persistence of ethnicity as a determinant in the perceptions of Italians is a direct outgrowth of structural separation. In addition, the American political system tends to encourage the persistence of Italian identification by its reliance on ethnic strategies.[7]

Out-group rejection leads to group uneasiness, which can only be pacified by individual or group advancement. Hence the Italian has a stake in the politics of recognition. The respondents in all groupings tended to prefer the Italian candidate rather than the non-Italian, regardless of party. The limited number of rewards available leads to inter-ethnic conflicts. Because the rewards at stake involve higher status rather than economic motives, the Italians' quest for rewards is transferred to one of seeking an intermediary, who serves as a protector and a symbolic recognition of the Italians' worth and dignity. It would follow that the higher the level of the position at stake, the more the Italians' need for recognition will be realized or go unfulfilled. Ethnicity as a determinant of political participation for Italians is most important on a local rather than on a national level.

The findings of other researchers seem to indicate that personal normlessness was characteristic of Italians. My findings do not support this contention. This might be because of changes in Italian society since these studies were undertaken. Perhaps the reason for the absence of personal normlessness, particularly among my immigrant respondents, is the impact of the American political and social system, which may have resulted in its neutralization. The movement of rural southern Italians to an urban America results in changes in family decision-making and discipline. The major determinants are length of city residence and inter-generational mobility. As one moves from the first to the third generation, decision-making and discipline are shared. Members of the family become increasingly independent. Also, family size declines gradually with length of city residence as one moves along the generational span. Immediate

---

7. Nathan Glazer and Daniel P. Moynihan, "How the Catholics Lost Out to the Jews in New York Politics," *New York Magazine* (August 1970).

family participation decreases from the first to the third generation, while extrafamilial participation increases. Thus, the changes in the family structure might indicate the Italians develop some links between the family, the Italian sub-society, and the larger society, resulting in the reduction of personal mistrust. My findings with regard to the impact of an urban environment on the Italian family structure support those of Palisi.[8] We find no evidence to substantiate the Horton and Thompson position of a clear relationship between social mistrust and political alienation.[9] There is an absence of perceived normlessness among the first-generation respondents. There is more definite evidence of political normlessness among those of the second- and third-generation respondents. The development of a shared decision-making arrangement among the second- and third-generation families is positively correlated with a decline in political powerlessness.

Those respondents whose occupational positions were much lower than their earlier personal or parental expectations were more likely to be politically alienated; moreover, those whose occupational and economic positions were the same or lower than those of their parents were more likely to feel politically powerless.

Marginal Catholics tended to be associated with high perceived political normlessness, while moderate Catholics, who were most often first- and second-generation Italians, were associated with high political powerlessness. A low socioeconomic position was positively correlated with a high sense of political powerlessness.

A sense of powerlessness is evident among the majority of the Italian immigrants interviewed and among a majority of the first- and second-generation respondents. There is a relative decline in such feelings among the third-generation

8. Palisi, "Patterns of Socio-Participation in Two Generations of Italian Americans."

9. Horton and Thompson, "Political Alienation as a Force in Political Action."

respondents, but are still evident. A majority of the respondents in the first- and second-generational groupings and some in the third see government as run by the "powerful." This aspect of political alienation supports the view of Lane that the political alienates believe that government serves some other set of interests than their own.[10] A majority of respondents among all generational groupings do not perceive government at any level as having any great impact on their daily lives. Similarly, a majority in all generational groupings felt that little could be done to ultimately change an unjust law. All suggested lower forms of political activity to bring about a change. A majority of Italian-Americans in all three groups tended to view government as too complicated to really understand. In addition, there is a low level of political information among a majority in all generational groupings. My findings support those of Almond and Verba, who found a positive correlation between low levels of political information and political alienation.[11] Regularity of voting behavior is also characteristic of a majority in all three groupings; however, the respondents in all groups did not see the act of voting as it related to the outcome of an election, or as making any difference.

In contrast to these findings, we find a decided absence of political powerlessness among all members of the control group. They do not see government as being run by the powerful, or understanding governmental affairs as a complicated matter. All of the control group see government as being responsive to their demands to change an unjust law. They also perceive government as having a much more significant impact on their daily lives than do the Italian-American respondents. All of the members of the control group do view the outcome of an election as making a difference.

A relative decline in political powerlessness in the third

10. Lane, *Political Ideology.*
11. Almond and Verba, *The Civic Culture.*

generation may be explained by a higher educational attainment and a relative increase in membership in the higher income and occupational categories. These characteristics among the second- and third-generation Italian-Americans would permit them better to perceive norm deviations than is the case with those to whom the political system is less familiar. My findings support those of Finfiter, who found a positive correlation between nativity and low political powerlessness.[12] The native-born Italian-American develops higher expectations regarding the behavior of public officials. The immigrants and first-generation respondents still feel the impact of their former political culture of "inner antagonism," which tends to stress a realistic and cynical image of government. With lower expectations, they may tend to be more tolerant of what they may perceive to be the far less frequent occurrence of norm violations.

I previously found political alienation to be associated with low levels of political interest, political participation, and organizational membership. Political interest was determined by frequency of political discussions, general interest in politics, interest in campaigns, and interest in specific elections. Political discussion among the politically alienated in all generational groupings was not high. The level of attention of those who followed accounts of politics rose as one moved from the first to the third generation, and interest in specific elections rose gradually along the same lines. The presence of Italian candidates in the mayoralty election of 1969 and a congressional primary in 1970 served to stimulate interest and political participation.

The interest level of the immigrant respondents seemed to be confined to the campaign and the act of voting. In general, there was an increase in interest level among the three groupings.

My findings that a relative increase in political interest

12. Finfiter, "Dimensions of Political Alienation."

occurs as one moves across the three-generational span do
not support the conclusions of Abbott. He found a correlation between a low level of political interest, political
apathy, and political participation.[13] I conclude that the low
interest level among the politically alienated Italian immigrants may be neutralized by the American political system,
in that political interest along the three-generational span
seems to increase independently of alienation. In contrast,
nearly all fifteen of the control group showed a high interest
level. A majority discussed politics frequently. They were
interested in political campaigns and specific elections.

Italians in lower socioeconomic categories tend to have
less economic security and feel less sense of control over
their political environment. My finding in this respect supports that of Lane.[14] The threat present in the politics of
the welfare state of deprivation of upper-strata Italian-
Americans may provide greater motivation for political participation than the promise of reward to the lower-SES Italian-Americans. Upper-strata Italian-Americans are more inclined toward increased political participation than those
in the lower strata. The social norms of upper-strata Italians
tend to emphasize political participation. Lower-strata Italian-Americans are more inclined to be influenced by the
cross-pressures of ethnic versus class identifications. Lower-
strata Italian-Americans are more likely to be politically
alienated; a low position in the social structure is interpreted
by them to mean inaccessibility to the means to achieved
desired ends—social, economic, and political—and hence his
exclusion from sharing in the dominant institutions, roles,
and values of American society. A clear residential, occupational, and income differentiation exists between the
members of the control group and the Italian-American
respondents in all groupings. Thus, no evidence is present

---

13. Abbott, "Political Alienation in Mexico and Italy."
14. Lane, *Political Life.*

of political alienation among the members of the control group, whose higher socioeconomic position allows greater access to the means to achieve desired ends.

I found no evidence to support the Horton and Thompson correlation between powerlessness and negative voting. In fact, those who felt politically powerless among the first- and second-generation respondents did not seem to be voting negatively on local issues. On both the national and local levels, I found no evidence to indicate that alienation was related to the respondents' party identification.

Generally speaking, the political activity of the respondents increases gradually as one moves from the first- to the third-generation respondents. I must add that this increase is not continuous and tends to be erratic. Ethnic candidates or specific issues may stir the Italian respondents to political action, but it is questionable how lasting its effect is, especially if the candidates are either defeated or stifled in their electoral bid. This kind of an experience may serve to reinforce alienated feelings in the form of further withdrawal and apathy.

I previously noted the absence of organizational membership when we move from the first- to the third-generation respondents. In fact, only three of the entire sample could be considered high organizational joiners. The organization to which the respondents belonged most frequently was a union or some other organization connected with their occupation. Party identification does not seem to have any independent relationship to low political alienation.

My focus on ethniclass views participation as an expression and outcome of an individual ethnic's integration into the political and social system. I implied that structural separation may result in pushing members of some ethnic groups to the margins of society and making access to the political process difficult, thereby decreasing the likelihood of their political participation. A structural separation tends to reinforce their predisposition not to participate. It may mean that the members of a particular ethniclass cannot receive or send a significant amount of political communication, or be active in many groups outside the subsociety. I found that the upper-SES Italians tend to vote Republican, while lower-SES Italians vote for the Democratic party on the national level. On the national level the Republican party may appeal to the upwardly mobile Italians, who are increasingly conscious of their class interests. On the national level, middle-income Italians tend to identify with the Republican party in periods of prosperity and with the Democratic party in times of severe economic stress.

The relationship between an increased level of political interests and political participation, and political alienation among the generational groupings seems to be strongest on the local level. Political alienation does not seem to have a great effect on the level of voter turnout, particularly in local elections. On the national level, the politically alienated among the respondents tended to be either politically indifferent or apathetic. The politically apathetic among the respondents do not see the American political system as a vehicle through which their needs and goals may be implemented. In addition, they do not see the connection between government's activities and their own lives. The politically apathetic do not perceive the act of voting or the joining of any organization as a means of improving their status.

On the local level, specific issues may provide the politically alienated among the Italians with specific objects and lead them to negative or protest voting. Appeals based on fulfilling the need for political power, or ethnic appeals based on the politics of recognition, may stir the Italians into greater political activity. Political powerlessness and political normlessness may interact in a populist type of candidate. In the New York mayoralty campaign, I do not think that the initial defeat of, and opposition to, John Lindsay was part of a backlash or built-in bigotry. I found a significant absence of ethnic, racial, and religious hostility among all the Italian respondents, including those who voted for Procaccino and Marchi. In the mayoralty campaign, what seemed to stir the respondents into political activity, aside from ethnicity, was a positive defense of acculturated values.

What impact does the political alienation of an ethnic group have on the American political system? The American political system does not tend toward the integration of some ethnic groups, and in fact it may systematically exclude some from sharing power. A structural separation excludes the politically alienated from participation. Though these people may have certain needs, they cannot see their becoming realized through the American political system. If the structural separation of ethnic groups is an accurate motif of America today, then this factor represents a potential destabilizing influence.

Some researchers contend that the national political system is insulated from the impact of the politically alienated. The political system on the national level inhibits negative sentiments from making their fullest impact since the political structure provides limited opportunities even for positive expressions to have effect on the system. The American party is cited as a means of deflecting alienated sentiments.

The American party system does seem to act as a vehicle for participation among the alienated. The party system is built on the acceptance of the "rules of the game." Both issue cleavages and procedural consensus result in the acceptance of the reality of political conflict. As a result, the politically alienated are not easily identifiable with one or the other party. The alienated have a choice of working within the parties and accepting the rules of the game or of presenting their alternatives outside the two parties. If the latter obtains, they remain fragmented and often ineffective. The alienated may be induced to remain on the margins of American politics and abandon politics or engage in ineffective or sporadic action. Based on this reasoning, one may hypothesize that the American parties may even attract the alienated. The Democratic party may project a working-class image. Those ethnics who are politically powerless may look to the Democratic party in an effort to achieve their goals. Those who are politically normless and do not like the way the government is presently operating may favor the Republican party because of its greater emphasis on individual and local responsibility in government and its opposition to many federal programs. These assertions must remain speculative and should be the subject of future study.

Those who uphold the insularity of the American political system from the effect of political alienation emphasize the survival and stability of the political system, not the quality of its performance. The lack of integration of ethnic groups in significant numbers into the political system does not augur well for the future of American democracy or for the quality of life in America. A Democratic political system, we assume, should attempt to extend satisfaction levels and its consensual base. The lack of integration of some ethnic groups results in the critical loss of counterbalancing in political activity; moreover, it does not permit the injection of new ideas and issues, or the recruitment of new talent vital to the growth of a democracy. In addition, the political system may not respond to legitimate needs.

If political needs and aspirations cannot be met on the national level, the structural separation of ethnic groups will tend to deflect their political activity to the local level, which is subject to negative and protest voting. Herein lies the potential destabilizing influence of political alienation among ethnic groups. The persistence of a structural separation may result in severe inter-ethnic and inter-racial tensions.

What I have said in earlier pages is that the core culture has held America together. It has been composed of a class of people who have controlled the institutions of American society.[15] The standard of what was America or an American has been its values and norms. The people were white and Protestant, and their institutions were English. American history was white-Anglo-Saxon-Protestant history. The men who analyzed and articulated American ideas were for the most part white Anglo-Saxon Protestants. They were the heart and mind of America. As Sal, an undertaker by profession, declared, "this group is especially anti-Italian. They think they own the country . . . that they are America. Everyone is considered a foreigner. They have no use for Italians since they are not considered as equal to them. The liberal President Wilson, a WASP, had a low opinion about Southern Europeans and Italians in particular."[16] That core society, then, has defined the place or role of ethnics, who were distinguished as Jews, Irishmen, Poles, Italians, Negroes, and so on.[17] If Wasps were alienated, it was because America had moved away from them, not because they regarded themselves as alien to the society or excluded from the social or political structure. As Bob, a first-generation printer, sarcastically put it, "They are the Americans . . . who fear mixing with anyone . . . particularly Italians."[18] The centers of the core society are easily identifiable, since they are essentially the institutions that are under attack today and are essentially on the defensive. As Mario, a young lawyer who seemed to battle to control his deep passions, said of them, "The Wasps . . . they are the establishment. They were the early settlers who are now exploiting all . . . including the Italians."[19] What is apparent is that, though the members of the core society still hold on to the centers of power, they do so with less legitimacy

---

15. E. Digby Baltzell, *The Protestant Establishment*, pp. 41–86.
16. Interview, Sal.
17. Warner and Srole, pp. 281–96.
18. Interview, Bob. See Baltzell, pp. 281–96.
19. Interview, Mario.

than in the past.[20] As Joe, a party activist, put it, "They hold the power. They definitely discriminate."[21] Antonio seemed to underscore this view, with "They got it all, power and money."[22] The previously unquestioned assumptions on which this power was based are seriously being challenged. The foundation of WASP dominance in national politics and culture rested on the supposition that WASPS were the true America, not any subculture or group.[23] Today, members of the core society need to enforce allegiance to something that their very place in power is supposed to make them take for granted.[24]

"Making it" in America has heretofore been defined according to the core society's values, and according to the assignment of roles by the social and political structure. Over the years, those "making it" did so on those terms. Those terms made the structure more responsive to other members of the core society. In America today, there is a growing realization of this arrangement, which is now being called into question, often in militant ways.[25] There is a growing realization among ethnics that they, in fact, have not "made it"; included among them are Blacks, Puerto Ricans, Poles, and Italians. As Paul, a first-generation respondent put it, "The WASPS came to escape persecution, yet they have in the past and are now doing the same thing to all minorities. They are negative and antagonistic to all foreigners who they regard as non-American. They have all the power and control over minority groups. They have the work skills . . . they prevent others from getting them . . . they use minorities against each other to keep their control. They are definitely unfavorable towards the

---

20. Baltzell, pp. 277–92, 315–35.
21. Interview, Joe.
22. Interview, Antonio.
23. Baltzell, pp. 46–86.
24. Ibid.
25. Ibid., pp. 277–93.

Italians."[26] Donato, a recent arrival, sensed this exclusion, too. "I have no contact with them. I have no opinion other than that they must be very influential since they were here very early."[27] Blacks are alienated because they have been out of the running in "making it." In turn, they do not understand the origin of the white ethnic's attitude. The Black wants what he thinks the whites are getting. One can get an inkling of this rising mood of exclusion from one commentator at the Urban Task Force of the U. S. Catholic Conferences:

> The ethnic American is sick of being stereotyped as a racist and dullard by phony white liberals, pseudo black militants and patronizing bureaucrats. . . . He pays the bill for every major governmental program and gets nothing or little in the way of return . . . he himself is the victim of class prejudice. . . . He has worked hard all his life to become a "good American" . . . [but] in many instances he is treated like the machine he operates.[28]

Another commentator declared, "Nobody has done anything for ethnics since Social Security. . . . Yet here they are being blamed for white racism. But they're not the people in the executive suites who would not hire a single Jew or Negro for so long."[29]

What is particularly awesome is the prospect that the inter-ethnic tension and conflict over the allocation of resources and rewards may take a more violent turn. Ethnic groups are competing for what are already scarce resources. Each ethnic group in its quest for status and power may not trust the other as the ruling class, or recognize the other's legitimacy. Ethnic groups are essentially in conflict as a result of the vacuum that is being created by the withdrawal of the Wasp from the centers of power, and by their

---

26. Interview, Paul.
27. Interview, Donato.
28. *New York Times,* June 17, 1970, p. 31.
29. Ibid.

inability to serve as effective mediators in the inter-ethnic dialogue. What is needed is an alliance of whites and Blacks, white-collar and blue-collar workers, based on mutual need and interdependence and hence an alliance of political participation. But before this can realistically come to pass, a number of ethnic groups have to develop in-group organization, identity, and unity. The Italian-Americans may prove to be a vital ingredient in not only forging that alliance but in serving as the cement that will hold our urban centers together.[30]

---

30. *Ibid.*, October 5, 1970, pp. 11, 21.

Questionnaire

Personal

Residence (to be asked of all respondents):
1. Are you married? How many children do you have?
2. Where were you born? In what year? (Be specific, town and province or city and state.)
   a. Repeat for wife.
3. What was the size of the town (unit—village, city) where you were born? How long did you live there? What was the predominant way people earned a living in this town? Who ran things in the town? Describe the different groups who lived there.
   a. How often did you visit large cities? How often did you watch television? How often did you attend the movies.
4. How long have you lived in this town (city)?
   a. Do you intend to stay in this town?
5. How long have you lived in this dwelling?
   a. Where did you live before you moved here? Why did you move here?

b. Do you have any member of your family living in this neighborhood? Town?

c. How often do you visit them? How often do they visit you?

6. How did you come to this city?

7. What was your impression of America while you were in Italy? How has that image or impression changed? Why?

Education:

8. What was the last grade you completed in school? Your father? Mother? Siblings?

9. How much time was spent in school discussing politics and current issues?

   a. Did you have an opportunity to discuss and express your opinions in such discussions?

Family:

10. What was your father's occupation?

    a. Were your parents dissatisfied with their economic situation?

    b. Who influenced you the most in your early years? In what ways?

11. How were decisions made in your family when you were a child?

    a. Who had the greater say (most voice) in making decisions in the family?

    b. Who exercised the discipline in the family?

    c. Who makes the decisions in *your* family now? (Immediate family.) How are they made? Who exercises the discipline?

12. How much influence did you or the other children have in family decisions?

13. (Repeat for own family.)

14. What can you recall about your father's political opinions? What party did he follow?

    a. Was politics discussed often at home? Do you recall any arguments?

    b. Did he express any likes or dislikes about candidates at election time?

    c. Did your mother vote as your father did? Who decided how they should vote?

15. Do you think your family influenced your outlook on politics?

16. Some people say that it's hardly fair to bring children into the world the way things look for the future. What is your opinion about this?

Religion:

17. (Hand Respondent Card)

    Which one of the following statements describes yourself?

    a. I don't believe in any religion.

    b. I am not a Catholic, but a . . .

    c. I am a believer, but not a Churchgoer.

    d. I go to Mass irregularly, but I believe.

    e. I go to Mass regularly.

    f. I receive Communion at least two or three times a year.

    g. I receive Communion at least once a month.

18. In general, how do you feel about religion? Is it important in your everyday life? Do you think about it often?

19. Have your attitudes or practices changed since your early years?

20. In what ways do you differ from your parents in your religious beliefs?

21. What are your thoughts about the Catholic Church?

    a. Some people say that the Church should speak its mind on politics. Do you agree?

    b. What do you think of the recent changes made in

the Church? Have there been too many changes?
Have they driven people away?

22. How do you think people in this community feel if a
person belongs to your religion?
23. How do you feel about people who belong to other
religions? Do you feel that they are different from you
in any way?
24. Does religion help a person to stay honest and keep him
on the right track, or doesn't it make much difference?
25. Do you have much contact with priests of your parish?
What has been the nature of your relationship with
them? (Repeat for Italy.)

Work, Satisfaction, Income:

26. What do you do for a living? Has this always been your
line of work? Are you happy with it?
27. Thinking back to the time when you were young, did
you ever have any special ambitions about what you
wanted to be?
    a. Have you had any special ambitions in recent years?
28. Did your parents have any special ideas or thoughts
about what you ought to be when you grew up?
29. What would you like your children to do when they
grow up?
30. Some people think that in spite of what others say, the
position of the average man is getting worse. Do you
agree?
31. Some people believe that a person has to live pretty
much for today and let tomorrow take care of itself. Do
you agree?
32. Economically, do you feel you are better off or worse
off today than in the past? Are you better off than your
parents were?
33. Did your parents have the opportunity to engage in a
different kind of living in Italy? (Repeat for U. S.) Do

you think that you had more of a chance to pursue a different job than your parents?

34. All things considered—income, advancement, opportunities—do you think it's satisfactory or not?
35. (Hand Respondent Card)
Please indicate the letter which comes closest to your income.

Class Identification:
36. Sometimes one hears the term "social class" as in middle class, or working class, etc. What do you think people mean by that term?
37. How important do you think social class is in the United States? In Italy?
38. Would you say you are of the upper class, middle, working, or lower class?
39. In what class are most of your friends?
40. To what class did your parents belong?
    a. To what class did they say they belonged?
41. How do your chances to improve your life compare with others in this country? Town? In Italy?
42. Think about your life today and your life as a child. Do you think there is a great difference? In what way is it different? Is life better or worse? What are the causes of these differences?

Trust—Friendship:
43. There are times a person really doesn't know who he can count on. Do you agree with this viewpoint? Are people more inclined to look out for themselves?
    a. Some people say that human nature is fundamentally selfish. Do you agree?
44. Some people say that most people can't be trusted and that if you don't watch out they will take advantage of you. Do you agree?

Acculturation, Assimilation, Ethnicity:

45. How do you think of yourself, as an Italian, Italian-American, or American?
    a. How do you feel other people think of you?
46. Do you feel closer to Italian or American ways of life? Why? Which has influenced the most?
47. Is there anything about yourself you consider particularly Italian? American?
    a. As you have grown older, have you become more or less interested in Italian things?
48. Would you consider your parents Italianized or Americanized? How would you describe them?
49. Which of these three groups do you like the best?
    a. Italians born and raised in Italy.
    b. Americans of Italian descent.
    c. Americans of non-Italian descent.
50. Do you think it helps a person to get ahead to be an Italian-American?
51. How do you think people generally in this country (repeat for city) feel about Italians? Do you think that there's much prejudice against Italians in this country (repeat for city)?
    If *yes:* a. What do you think is responsible for it?
             b. Are there any particular groups prejudiced against the Italians?
52. Have you ever felt discriminated against because of your nationality?
53. Some people have complained that T.V., radio, etc., are giving their gangster characters Italian names. Have you been aware of this? Would you consider this a form of prejudice?
54. Do you think there is any truth to the view that most big gangsters and racketeers in this country are of Italian descent? Why?
55. How do you feel about words like guinea or wop? Has

anyone ever called you by these words? If so, who? How did you feel about it?

56. What has been the nationality of your present and past friends?

57. What were the nationalities of the people living in the various neighborhoods in which you have lived? Are living in now?
(Both groups.)
a. Is there anything you like or dislike about these groups? Have your feelings changed over the years?

58. Have you ever thought of changing your name so that it would not be taken for Italian? What is your opinion of such changes? (Both.)

59. How do you feel about your children marrying a non-Italian? Did you ever feel differently?

60. When you come across an Italian name in the newspaper or in everyday life, are you aware that the name is Italian?

61. Do you often try to gauge the nationalities of people?
a. For what clues do you look?

62. Do you think it sometimes helps to understand other people if you know their national origins?

63. How do you feel about people with national origins different from yours?

64. People have varying opinions about different nationalities. How do you feel about the following?
a. Old time Americans—Yankees.
b. Jews.
c. Negroes.
d. Irish.
e. Germans.
f. Puerto Ricans.

65. Are you glad or sorry about seeing Italians mixed in with people of other nationalities in this country?
a. Have you ever felt differently?

66. If you had your way, which would you like best: to

live in an Italian neighborhood or a mixed one?

67. How do you think you would feel if you went back to Italy? Would you feel at home? Have you ever returned to Italy? Do you intend to return? Why would you return?

68. Are you ever homesick for Italy?

69. Would you like to spend the rest of your life in the United States?

    a. Are you satisfied with your life in the U. S.?

70. Suppose you could live in Italy as well as you live here. Would you want to go back?

71. Do you write regularly to friends or relatives in Italy?

    a. Do you send money or packages to your friends or relatives in Italy?

72. When someone tells you a price in U. S. dollars, do you ever translate it mentally to Italian liras?

73. Which do you prefer to eat most of the time, American or Italian-style food?

74. Do you read Italian? Do you ever read Italian newspapers?

    a. What interests you most in such papers?

75. Do you speak Italian? How often? With whom?

    a. Do you like speaking it?

    If *no,* would you like to learn?

76. Do your children speak it?

    a. Would you like them to learn it?

    b. Do you want them to be interested in Italian ways?

77. Do you like speaking English?

78. Do you follow any sports or events associated with Italy, e.g., soccer, opera?

79. Did you ever find yourself rooting for the Italian in sports or politics or something like that?

80. If an Italian team came to the U. S. to play an American team, which would you want to win?

81. If you had to choose between two men of equal ability or had no political difference, and one was of Italian

descent and the other non-Italian, for whom would you vote?

82. Are you interested in seeing Italian-Americans get ahead in politics?

83. Do you feel most Italians are Democrats or Republicans?
    a. If Democrats—suppose the Italians were running on the Republican ticket and the non-Italians on the Democratic ticket, which would you vote for?
    b. Reverse if they choose Republican.

84. In what class do you think most people of Italian descent belong?

85. In the last twenty years do you think that most people of Italian descent bettered themselves in jobs, education, the professions, etc.? Why is this so?

86. In general, how does your life now compare with your life in Italy?

Ideology and Issues:

87. In general, are you interested in politics? Have you ever been interested in the politics of Italy?

88. How would you describe yourself, liberal, conservative, etc.?

89. One sometimes hears that some people have so much influence and power over the way government is run that the majority are ignored. Do you agree? Are there any groups or individuals you believe have too much power? (Town, country—U. S., Italy).

90. What do you think are the major problems facing America today? Italy? What is the most important problem?
    a. What should the individual do about them?

91. I'm going to read off a list of problems and issues. Tell me how you feel about each.
    a. Student protests
    b. Vietnam
    c. Democracy
    d. Labor unions

e. Italy's constitution
f. Segregation and Negroes
g. Communism and Russia
h. Guaranteed annual income
i. Welfare programs, anti-poverty, etc.
j. Socialism
k. Fascism

92. Are you able to identify the senators from your state, Congressmen from your district, the Secretary of State?
    a. (For Italian Respondents)
    Can you name the President and Prime Minister of Italy? The representatives to the Senate and Chamber of Deputies from your district and province?

93. I'm going to name some men who have been prominent in Italian political history. What is your opinion of them?
    (For Italian Respondents)
    a. Togliatti
    b. Pietro Nenni
    c. Alcide De Gasperi
    d. Benito Mussolini
    e. Enrico Mattei
    f. Pope John
    g. Aldo Moro
    h. Gabrielle D'Annunzio
    i. Orlando
    j. Victorio Emmanuel
    k. Pope Pius

Political Discussion–Information:

94. Have you talked politics with anyone recently? What was the nature of the discussion?

95. Do you ever discuss politics with friends or relatives?
    a. Are you active in such discussions?
    If *no*, why do you avoid such discussion?

96. Are there some people with whom you definitely wouldn't discuss politics?

97. Is there anyone today whose opinions on politics you particularly admire, e.g., friends? Especially dislike?

98. Have there been any big changes in your opinions in the past years?

99. Do you follow accounts of politics regularly in the newspapers, T.V., etc.? (Also for Italians in Italy, or since coming to U. S.)

100. How well do you think you understand important national, international issues facing the U. S.? Italy? Local?

101. Some people say that politics and government are so complicated that the average man can't really understand what is going on. Do you agree? Why is this so?
    a. Suppose an issue arose that might affect your way of life but you didn't understand it. What would you do to find out more about it?

Political Efficacy:

102. Who do you say runs the national government?

103. Do people like you have much to say about what government does?

104. Suppose a regulation were being considered by (town, village, Congress, Parliament) that you considered unjust or harmful. What do you think you could do?

105. If such a situation arose, how likely is it that you would do something about it?

106. If you made an effort to change it, would you be successful?

107. Some say that there is little use in writing to politicians since they are not really interested in the problems of the average man. Do you agree?

108. Are strikes of any real political benefit?

109. How much effect do the activities of the government in Washington have on your everyday life?
    a. Do such activities tend to improve conditions in the country?

110. Have local governments (town, state, village, or province) helped you in any way?
111. If you were to talk to a politician about an issue, do you think you would be given equal treatment?
112. If you explained your point of view to a government official, what effect do you think it would have?

Organizations–Membership–Political Party:

113. Did you belong to any organizations, political or otherwise, such as clubs, unions, etc.? Do you now belong to any organizations?
    a. Were you ever an officer in them? Did you attend the meetings?
    b. What satisfaction did you get from being a member?
114. Are you now a member of any political party or support one?
    a. Are your friends or relatives?
    b. Do all your friends support the same party?
115. Do you vote regularly? How often? Were there times you didn't vote? Why? What was your first occasion to vote?
116. How do you feel when you go to vote? Which party do you normally vote for?
117. Do you pay much attention to campaigning? Is it needed or would we be better off without it? Do you ever get angry at something in the campaign?
    a. All candidates sound good in their speeches, but you can never tell what they will do after they are elected. Do you agree with this viewpoint?
118. Could you name the major parties in Italy? U. S.? Could you name the party leaders? (Only for Italian parties.)
119. What is your reaction when a politician says he wants to be elected because it's his obligation to help his people?

120. Can you think of any election in which you were particularly interested?

121. Why did you decide to join the x party (or vote for it) ? Why do you prefer it over the others?

122. Are there any differences between political parties? Does one party favor one group or class and another party favor another group or class?

123. Can you remember how you voted in the Presidential elections (general elections) as far back as you can?

124. (For Italian Respondents list all parties) Suppose the Communist party controlled the national government. Do you think its policies and activities would seriously endanger the welfare of the country or certain groups or individuals?

125. Why do you think the Communist and Socialist parties are so strong in Italy? Why is this not the case in the U.S.?

126. Suppose your son or daughter decided to marry someone of the Socialist party (go through list), would you be pleased?

127. Do you think the outcome of an election makes any difference in how you and your family are getting along? Does your vote make a difference?

128. Have you ever done any of the following?
    a. Spoken to someone in office on an issue.
    b. Written a letter on an issue in political office.
    c. Gone to a political rally.
    d. Asked people to vote for one candidate over another.
    e. Worked for a candidate.
    f. Led or took part in a protest demonstration.
    g. Taken part in a strike.

129. Where is all this turmoil and unrest leading? (Both for Italy and U. S.) What is Italy's future? America's?
    a. Will there be any major change in who runs the country? Which groups or individuals will run the country in ten years? Will this be an improvement over what exists now?

Bibliography

Documents

Italy: Documents & Notes. *Italian Emigration: Some Aspects. International Agreements* (November–December, 1965).

Italy: Emigration Report #35. *Italian Emigration Over a Century: Various Aspects and Characteristics* (Rome: March–April, 1962).

National Bureau of Economic Research. *International Migration* (Washington, 1929, Vols. 1 and 2).

Ninth Annual Statistical Guide for New York City (Department of Commerce and Industrial Development, 1965).

U. S. Bureau of Census. *Population,* 1960, Part 1, 24, 32, 33, 34.

Dissertations–Theses

Abbott, David. "Political Alienation in Mexico & Italy." Ph.D. Dissertation, University of North Carolina.

Butera, Joseph. "A Study of the Italo American Dialect: Adaptations into the Italian Language or Dialects for the Purpose of Adjustment in an Italian American Environment." M.A. Thesis, New York University, 1941.

Dyson, James. "Political Alienation: A Study of Apathy, Discontent and Dissidence." Ph.D. dissertation, Indiana University, 1964.

Matthews, M. F. "The Role of the Public School in the Assimilation of the Italian Immigrant in New York City." Ph.D. dissertation, Fordham University, 1966.

Mondello, Salvatore. "The Italian Immigrant in Urban America 1880–1920." Ph.D. dissertation, New York University, 1960.

Parenti, Michael. "Ethnic and Political Attitudes: Three Generations of Italian Americans." Ph.D. dissertation, Harvard University, 1950.

Polizzi, J. A. "Southern Italian Society: Its Peasantry and Change." Ph.D. dissertation, Cornell University, 1968.

Rossili, V. R. "A Study of the Effect of Transplantation Upon the Attitudes of Southern Italians in New York City as Revealed by Survivors of the Mass Migration 1887–1915." Ph.D. dissertation, New York University, 1967.

Sangree, Walter H. "Mel Hyblaeum: A Study of the People of Middletown of Sicilian Extraction." M.A. Thesis, Wesleyan University, 1952.

Tait, Joseph W. "Some Aspects of the Effect of the Dominant American Culture Upon the Children of Italian Born Parents." M.A. Thesis, Teachers College, Columbia, 1942.

Books

Adams, John and Barile, Paolo. *The Government of Republican Italy*. Boston: Houghton Mifflin, 1961.

Adorno, T. W. *The Authoritarian Personality*. New York: Harper, 1950.

Albrecht-Carrie, René. *Italy: From Napoleon to Mussolini*. New York: Columbia University Press, 1950.

Almond, Gabriel and Verba, Sidney. *The Civic Culture*. Princeton: Princeton University Press, 1963.

Backstrom, Charles and Marsh, Gerald. *Survey Research*. Chicago: Northwestern University Press, 1963.

Bailey, Harry and Katz, Ellis. *Ethnic Group Politics*. Columbus, Ohio: Merrill Publishing Co., 1969.

Baltzell, Digby E. *The Protestant Establishment*. New York: Random House, 1964.

Banfield, Edward C. *The Moral Basis of a Backward Society*. Glencoe, Ill.: The Free Press, 1958.

———— and Wilson, James Q. *City Politics*. Cambridge, Mass.: Harvard University Press, 1966.

Barrie, W. D. *Italians and Germans in Australia: A Study of*

Assimilation. Melbourne: Australian National University, 1954.

Barzini, Luigi. *The Italians.* New York: Atheneum, 1965.

Blauner, Robert. *Alienation and Freedom.* Chicago: University of Chicago Press, 1964.

Brandenburg, Broughton. *Imported Americans.* New York: Fred Stokes Co. Publishers, 1904.

Bucci, Vincent. *Chiesa e Stato.* The Hague: Martinus Nijhoff, 1969.

Campbell, Angus *et al. The Voter Decides.* Evanston, Ill.: Row, Peterson Co., 1954.

————. *The American Voter.* New York: John Wiley, 1960.

Child, Irwin. *Italian or American?* New Haven: Yale University Press, 1943.

Cingari, Gaetano. *Il Mezzogiorno e Giustono Fortunato.* Florence: Parenti, 1954.

Cilento, Nicola. *Italian meridionali longoburda.* Milan: R. Riccardi, 1966.

Cohen, Albert. *Deviance and Control.* Englewood Cliffs, N. J.: Prentice Hall, 1966.

Covello, Leonard. *The Social Background of the Italo American School Child.* Leiden: E. J. Brill, 1967.

DeGrazia, Sebastian. *The Political Community: A Study in Anomie.* Chicago: University of Chicago Press, 1948.

DiPalma, Giuseppe. *Apathy and Mass Participation.* Berkeley, Calif.: University of California Press, 1966.

Di Renzo, Gordon. *Personality, Power and Politics.* South Bend, Indiana: Notre Dame University Press.

Dogan, Mattei and Petracca, O. *Parti politici e strutture sociali in Italia.* Milan: Edizioni di Communita, 1968.

Dolci, Danilo. *Report From Palermo.* New York: Orien Press, 1956.

Domhoff, William G. *Who Rules America?* Englewood Cliffs, N. J.: Prentice Hall, 1967.

Dore, Grazia. *La democrazia Italiana e l'emigrazione in America.* Brescia: Morcelliani, 1964.

Eisenstadt, S. N. *The Absorption of Immigrants.* London: Routledge & Kegan Paul Ltd., 1954.

Ellis, John R. *American Catholicism.* Chicago: University of Chicago Press, 1956.

Federal Writers Project. *The Italians of New York.* New York: WPA, 1936.

Foerester, Robert. *The Italian Immigration of Our Times.* Cambridge, Mass.: Harvard University Press, 1919.

Femminella, Frank. *Power and Class: The Italian-American Experience.* Staten Island, N. Y.: The American-Italian Historical Association, 1973.

Fromm, Erich. *The Sane Society.* New York: Rinehart and Holt, 1955.

Fuchs, Lawrence, ed. *American Ethnic Politics.* New York: Harper & Row, 1968.

Galasso, Giuseppe. *Mezzogiorno medievale e moderno.* Torino: Einuadi, 1965.

Galli, Giorgio and Prandi, Alfonso. *Patterns of Political Participation in Italy.* New Haven: Yale University Press, 1970.

Galtung, Johan. *Members of Two Worlds: Development in Three Villages in Sicily.* New York: Columbia University Press, 1970.

Gans, Herbert. *The Urban Villagers.* New York: The Free Press, 1962.

Gerimino, Dante. *The Government & Politics of Contemporary Italy.* New York: Harper & Row, 1968.

Gerson, Louis. *The Hyphenate in Recent American Politics and Diplomacy.* Lawrence, Kansas: University of Kansas Press, 1964.

Glazer, Nathan and Moynihan, Daniel P. *Beyond the Melting Pot.* Cambridge, Mass.: Harvard University Press, 1963.

Gordon, Milton. *Social Class in American Sociology.* New York: McGraw Hill Book Co. Inc., 1963.

―――. *Assimilation in American Life.* New York: Oxford University Press, 1964.

Grasso, Pier Giovanni. *Personalita Giovaniti in Tranzione: Dal Familismo al Personalismo.* Aurich: Pas Verlag, 1964.

Greeley, Andrew. *Why Can't They Be Like Us?* New York: E. P. Dutton, 1971.

Handlin, Oscar. *Boston's Immigrants. A Study in Acculturation.* Cambridge, Mass.: Harvard University Press, 1959.

————. *The Uprooted*. Boston: Little Brown, 1951.

————. *Race and Nationality in American Life*. New York: Doubleday & Co., Inc., 1957.

Hansen, Morris et al. *Sample Survey Methods and Theory*. New York: John Wiley, 1953.

Hauser, Philip, ed. *Handbook for Social Research in Urban America*. UNESCO, 1965.

Hingham, John. *Strangers in the Land*. New York: Atheneum, 1963.

Hyman, Sidney. *Political Socialization*. New York: The Free Press, 1953.

Jemolo, A. C. *Church and State in Italy*. Oxford: Beachurd, 1960.

Keniston, Kenneth. *The Uncommitted Youth: Alienated Youth in American Society*. New York: Harcourt, Brace and World, Inc., 1966.

Kent, M. and Zeigler, Harmon. *The Electoral Process*. Englewood Cliffs, N. J.: Prentice Hall, 1966.

Kogan, Norman. *A Political History of Postwar Italy*. New York: Praeger, 1966.

Kornhauser, Arthur. *The Politics of the Mass Society*. Glencoe, Ill.: The Free Press, 1959.

Lane, Robert. *Political Ideology*. Glencoe, Ill.: The Free Press, 1962.

La Palombara, Joseph. *Interest Groups in Italian Politics*. Princeton, N. J.: Princeton University Press, 1964.

Levin, Murray and Blackwood, Charles. *The Alienated Voter*. Holt, Rinehart & Winston, 1960.

Litchfield, Edward H. *Voting Behavior in a Metropolitan Area*. Ann Arbor, Mich.: University of Michigan Press, 1941.

LoPreato, Joseph. *Peasants No More*. Calif.: Chandler, 1967.

————. *Italian-Americans*. New York: Random House, 1970.

Mariano, John. *The Second Generation of Italians in New York*. New York: Christopher Publishing House, 1921.

Marvick, Dwaine and Nixon, Charles, ed. *Political Decision Maker*. Glencoe, Ill.: The Free Press, 1961.

Merton, Thomas. *Social Theory and Social Structure*. Glencoe, Ill.: Free Press, 1957.

Milbrath, Lester W. *Political Participation*. Chicago: Rand McNally and Co., 1965.

Miller, Stuart. *The Unwelcome Immigrant: The American Image of the Chinese 1785–1882.* Berkeley, Calif.: University of California Press, 1969.

Musatti, Riccardi. *La via del sud.* Milan: Edizioni di Communita, 1955.

Neuman, Franz. *The Democratic and the Authoritarian State.* Glencoe, Ill.: The Free Press, 1957.

Nisbet, Robert. *The Sociological Tradition.* New York: Basic Books, 1966.

Novak, Michael. *Rise of the Unmeltable Ethnics.* New York: Macmillan Co., 1972.

Paulson, Belden and Ricci, Athos. *The Searchers.* Chicago: Quadrangle Books, 1966.

Pisani, Lawrence. *The Italians in America.* New York: Exposition Press, 1957.

Pye, Lucian. *Political Culture and Political Development.* Princeton, N. J.: Princeton University Press.

Redford, Robert. *Peasant Society and Culture.* Chicago: University of Chicago Press, 1956.

Rose, Arnold. *The Power Structure.* New York: Oxford University Press, 1967.

Salvadori, Massimo. *Italy.* Englewood Cliffs, N. J.: Prentice Hall, Inc., 1965.

Schermerhorn, R. A. *Comparative Ethnic Relations: A Framework for Theory and Research.* New York: Random House, 1970.

Scotellaro, Rocco. *Contadini del sud.* Bari: Laterza, 1954.

Schragg, Peter. *The Decline of the Wasp.* New York: Simon & Schuster, 1970.

Shibutani, Tomatsu and Kwan, Kiav. *Ethnic Stratification.* New York: Macmillan Co., 1965.

Sjoberg, Gideon and Nett, Roger. *A Methodology for Social Research.* New York: Harper & Row, 1968.

Smith, Dennis Mack. *Italy: A Modern History.* Ann Arbor, Mich.: University of Michigan Press, 1969.

Tarrow, Sidney. *Peasant Communism in Southern Italy.* New Haven: Yale University Press, 1967.

Viterbo, Michele. *Il sud e l'unita: genti del sud.* Bari: Laterza, 1966.

Warner, W. L. *Social Class in America.* New York: Harper & Row, 1960.

Warner, Lloyd and Srole, Leo. *The Social Systems of American Ethnic Groups.* New Haven: Yale University Press, 1945.

Wattenberg, Ben. *This is USA.* New York: Doubleday & Co., 1965.

Whyte, William. *Street Corner Society.* Chicago: University of Chicago Press, 1955.

Williams, Phyllis. *South Italian Folkways in Europe and America.* New Haven: Yale University Press, 1938.

Williams, Robin M., Jr. *Strangers Next Door.* Englewood Cliffs, N. J.: Prentice Hall Inc., 1964.

Articles

Abscarian, G. and Stanage, S. "Alienation and the Radical Right." *Journal of Politics* (November 1966).

Agger, Robert, et al. "Political Cynicism: Measurement and Meaning." *Journal of Politics* (August 1961).

Aho, William. "Ethnic Mobility in Northeastern United States: An Analysis of Census Data." *The Sociological Quarterly* (Fall 1969).

Allinsmith, Wesley and Allinsmith, Beverly. "Religious Affiliation and Political Economic Attitude: A Study of Eight Major U. S. Religious Groups." *Public Opinion Quarterly* (Fall 1948).

Appel, John. "American Negro and Immigrant Experiences: Similarities and Differences." *American Quarterly* (1968).

Breton, R. "Institutional Completeness of Ethnic Communities and the Personal Relations of Immigrants." *American Journal of Sociology* (September 1964).

Browning, Charles. "On the Meaning of Alienation." *American Sociological Review* (1966).

Bruce, J. M. "Intragenerational Occupational Mobility and Visiting with Kin and Friend." *Social Forces* (September 1970).

Bugleski, B. R. "Assimilation Through Intermarriage." *Social Forces* (December 1961).

Campisi, Paul J. "Ethnic Family Patterns: The Italian Family in the U. S." *American Journal of Sociology* 53 (1948).

Cezareo, Vincenzo. "Immigrati e Associocizionismi voluntario." *Study Emigrazione* (October 1966).

Clark, J. P. "Measuring Alienation Within a Social System." *American Sociological Review* (December 1959).

Cornwell, Elmer. "Party Absorption of Ethnic Groups: The Case of Providence, Rhode Island." *Social Forces* (March 1960).

Crespi, Leo. "The Cheater Problem in Polling." *Public Opinion Quarterly* (1945).

Darroch, Gordon and Marsten, Wilfred. "Ethnic Differentiation: Ecological Aspects of a Multidimensional Concept." *International Migration Review* (Fall 1963).

Dean, D. G. "Alienation and Political Apathy." *Social Forces* (March 1960).

————. "Alienation: Its Meaning and Measurement." *American Sociological Review* (October 1961).

Dillingham, Harry C. "Protestant Religion and Social Status." *American Journal of Sociology* (January 1965).

DiRenzo, Gordon. "Professional Politicians and Personality Structure." *American Journal of Sociology* (September 1967).

Dowhrend, B. and Smith, R. J. "Toward a Theory of Acculturation." *Southwest Journal of Anthropology* (1963).

Duncan, Otis and Lieberson, Stan. "Ethnic Segregation and Assimilation." *American Journal of Sociology* (January 1959).

Eckhardt, K. W. and Hendershot, G. "Transformation of Alienation into Public Opinion." *Sociological Quarterly* (Autumn 1967).

Etzioni, Amitai. "The Ghetto—a Re-Evaluation." *Social Forces* (March 1959).

Evans, Franklin. "On Interview Cheating." *Public Opinion Quarterly* (Spring 1961).

Femminella, Francis X. "The Impact of Italian Migration and American Catholicism." *The American Catholic Sociological Review* (Fall 1961).

Finfiter, Ada. "Dimensions of Political Alienation." *American Political Science Review* (June 1970).

Fitzpatrick, Joseph. "The Importance of Community in the Process of Immigrant Assimilation." *International Migration Review* (Fall 1966).

Fried, R. C. "Urbanization and Italian Politics." *Journal of Politics* (August 1967).

Gallo, Patrick J. "Student Alienation at an American University." *Rassegna Italiana di Sociologia* (April–June 1970).

———. "Ethnicity and Socio-Political Preferences: The Jews of New York City." *Rassegna Italiana di Sociologia* (April–June 1973).

Gerson, William M. "Alienation in Mass Society." *Sociology and Social Research* (January 1965).

Gilky, G. R. "The U. S. and Italy: Migration and Repatriation." *The Journal of Developing Areas* (October 1967).

Glazer, Nathan and Moynihan, Daniel. "How the Catholics Lost Out to the Jews in New York Politics," *New York Magazine* (August 1970).

Gleason, Phillip. "The Melting Pot: Symbol of Fusion or Confusion?" *American Quarterly* (Spring 1964).

Goertzel, Ted. "A Note on Status Crystallization and Urbanization." *Social Forces* (September 1970).

Gordon, Daniel. "Immigrants and Urban Governmental Forms in American Cities, 1933–1960." *American Journal of Sociology* (September 1968).

Hastings, Philip and Hoge, Dean. "Religious Change Among College Students Over Two Decades." *Social Forces* (September 1970).

Hazelrigg, L. "Religious and Class Bases of Political Conflict in Italy." *American Journal of Sociology* (January 1970).

Heiss, Jerold. "Residential Segregation and the Assimilation of the Italians in an Australian City." *International Migration Review* (1966).

———. "Factors in Immigrant Assimilation." *Social Forces* (June 1969).

Heller, Celia. "Class as an Expression of Ethnic Differences in Mobility Aspirations." *International Migration Review* (Fall 1967).

Hodge, Robert and Treiman, Don. "Class Identification in the U. S." *American Journal of Sociology* (March 1968).

Ianni, Francis. "Residence and Occupational Mobility: The Italian American Colony in Norristown." *Social Forces* (October 1957).

———. "The Italo-American Teenager." *The Annals* (November 1961).

―――. "Time and Place Variables in Acculturation Research."
American Anthropologist (February 1958).

Jansen, Clifford. "Leadership in the Toronto Italian Ethnic
Group." *International Migration Review* (Fall 1966).

Jaros, Dean et al. "The Malevolent Leader: Political Socialization
in an American Subculture." *The American Political Science
Review* (June 1968).

Kantrowitz, Nathan. "Ethnic and Racial Segregation in the New
York Metropolitan Area, 1960." *American Journal of Sociology* (May 1969).

Keniston, Kenneth. "Alienation and the Decline of Utopia."
American Scholar (Spring 1960).

Kennedy, Ruby Jo. "Single or Triple Melting Pot? Intermarriage
Trends in New Haven, 1870–1940." *American Journal of
Sociology* (January 1944).

Kon, Igor. "The Concept of Alienation in Modern Sociology."
Social Research (Fall 1967).

Krickus, Richard. "The White Ethnic: Who Are They and
Where Are They Going?" *City Magazine* (June 1971).

Lehrman, N. S. "On Alienation: Two Contrasting Views." *Science and Society* (Summer 1961).

Levin, Murray. "Political Strategy for the Alienated Voter."
Public Opinion Quarterly (Spring 1962).

Litt, Edgar. "Political Cynicism and Political Futility." *Journal
of Politics* (May 1963).

Lopreato, Joseph. "Economic Development and Cultural Change."
Human Organization (Fall 1962).

―――. "Social Mobility in Italy." *American Journal of Sociology*
(November 1965).

―――. "Upward Social Mobility and Political Orientations."
Amercan Sociological Review (August 1967).

MacDonald, John and MacDonald, Lentrice. "Urbanization,
Ethnic Group, and Social Segmentation." *Social Research*
(Winter 1962).

Mailey, Hugo. "The Italian Vote in Philadelphia, 1928–46."
Public Opinion Quarterly (Spring 1950).

Meir, Dorothy and Windell, Bill. "Anomia and Differential Access to the Achievement of Life's Goals." *American Sociological Review* (February 1966).

Miller, S. M. "The Participant Observer and Over-Rapport." *American Sociological Review* (August 1952).

Miranda, Giulio. "From the Italo Think Tank." *Italo-American Times* (September 1972).

Mizruchi, E. H. "Social Structure and Anomie in a Small City." *American Sociological Review* (April 1961).

Moss, Leonard and Thompson, Walter. "The South Italian Family: Literature and Observation." *Human Organization* (Spring, 1969).

———— and Cappannari, Stephen. "Estate and Class in a South Italian Hill Village." *American Anthropologist* (1962).

Naegle, K. "Attachment and Alienation." *American Journal of Sociology* (May 1958).

Nahirny, V. C. and Fishman, J. A. "American Immigrant Group: Ethnic Identification and the Problem of Generation." *Sociological Review* (November 1965).

Nam, C. B. "Nationality Groups and Social Stratification in America." *Social Forces* (May 1959).

Natanson, Maurice. "Alienation and Social Role." *Social Research* (Autumn 1966).

Neal, Arthur and Rettig, Salamon. "Dimensions of Alienation Among Manual and Non-Manual Workers." *American Sociological Review* (August 1963).

Nelli, Humbert. "Italians in Urban America: A Study in Ethnic Adjustment." *International Review* (Summer 1967).

Netler, G. "A Measure of Alienation." *American Sociological Review* (December 1957).

Ollman, Bertell. "Marx's Use of Class." *American Journal of Sociology* (March 1968).

Olsen, M. E. "Alienation and Public Opinion." *Public Opinion Quarterly* (Summer 1965).

Palisi, B. J. "Ethnic Generation and Family Structure." *Journal of Marriage and the Family* (Fall 1966).

————. "Patterns of Socio-Participation in Two Generations of Italian Americans." *Sociological Quarterly* (Spring 1966).

Parenti, Michael. "Ethnic Politics and the Persistence of Ethnic Identification." *American Political Science Review* (September 1967).

Plaux, M. "On Studying Ethnicity." *Public Opinion Quarterly* (Spring 1972).

Pope, Liston. "Religion and Class Structure." *Annals of the American Academy of Political and Social Science* (March 1948).

Powers, M. G. "Class, Ethnicity and Residence in Metropolitan America." *Demography* (1968).

Price, Charles. "Southern Europeans in Australia: Problems of Assimilation." *International Migration Review* (Summer 1968).

Psathas, G. "Ethnicity, Social Class and Independence from Parental Control." *American Sociological Review* (August 1957).

Rhodes, Lewis. "Anomia, Aspirations and Status." *Social Forces* (May 1964).

Richardson, Alan. "A Theory and A Method for the Psychological Study of Assimilation." *International Migration Review* (Fall 1967).

———— and Taft, Ronald. "Australian Attitudes Toward the Immigrant: A Review of Social Survey Findings." *International Migration Review* (Summer 1968).

Reis Powel, Alan. "Differentials in the Integration Process of Dutch and Italian Immigrants in Edmonton, Canada." *International Review* (1966).

Robinson, W. S. "The Motivational Structure of Participation." *American Sociological Review* (1952).

Rosen, Bernard. "Race Ethnicity and the Achievement Syndrome." *American Sociological Review* (February 1959).

Rosenthal, Erich. "Acculturation Without Assimilation?: The Jewish Community of Chicago, Illinois." *American Journal of Sociology* (November 1960).

Russo, Nicholas. "Three Generations of Italians in New York City: Their Religious Acculturation." *The International Review* (Spring 1969).

Schachter, G. "Rural Life in South Italy." *American Journal of Economics* (October 1965).

Schermerhorn, R. A. "Toward a General Theory of Minority Groups." *Phylon* (Fall 1964).

Scott, M. B. and Turner, R. "Weber and the Anomic Theory of Deviance." *Sociological Quarterly* (Summer 1965).

Seeman, Melvin. "On the Personal Consequences of Alienation in Work." *American Sociological Review* (April 1967).

Sewell, William and Shah, Vimal. "Social Class, Parental Encouragement and Educational Aspirations." *American Journal of Sociology* (March 1968).

Silverman, Sydel. "Prestige in a Central Italian Community." *American Anthropologist* (August 1966).

———. "Amoral Familism Reconsidered." *American Anthropologist* (Fall 1968).

Simmons, Melvin. "On the Meaning of Alienation." *American Sociological Review* (December 1959).

———. "Alienation, Membership and Political Knowledge." *Public Opinion Quarterly* (Fall 1969).

Strodtbeck, Fred et al. "Evaluation of Occupation: A Reflection of Jewish and Italian Mobility Differences." *American Sociological Review* (October 1957).

Tarrow, Sidney. "Political Dualism and Italian Communism." *American Political Science Association* (March 1967).

Templeton, F. "Alienation and Political Participation." *Public Opinion Quarterly* (Summer 1966).

Thompson, W. E. and Horton, J. E. "Political Alienation as a Force in Political Action." *Social Forces* (March 1960).

Veccoli, Rudolph. "Peasants and Prelates." *Journal of Social History* (Spring 1969).

———. "Contadini in Chicago: A Critique of the Uprooted." *Journal of American History* (December 1964).

Velikonja, Joseph. "Italian Immigrants in the U. S. in the Mid-Sixties." *International Migration Review* (Summer 1967).

Williams, Fred W. "Recent Voting Behavior of Some Nationality Groups." *American Political Science Association* (June 1964).

Wispe, Lauren and Thayer, Paul. "Some Methodological Problems in the Analysis of the Unstructured Interview." *Public Opinion Quarterly* (1954).

Wolfinger, Raymond. "The Development and Persistence of Ethnic Voting Group." *American Political Science Review* (December 1965).

Zenger, Milton. "Social Forces Involved in Group Identification and Withdrawal." *Daedalus* (Spring 1961).

Index

Abbott, David, 147, 179, 180, 201.
See also Italy, Italians, Italian-Americans, political alienation
Abegglen, J. C., 35. *See also* alienation, anomie, Italians, Italian-Americans
Aberbach, Joel, 30, 31, 38, 39, 40. *See also* alienation, anomie, political alienation
Abscarian, Gilbert, 34, 35. *See also* alienation, anomie
acculturation, 21, 24, 27, 118, 123–24, 194, 215–17; definition, 21. *See also* assimilation, ethnicity, food, Oscar Handlin, Jerold Heiss, Italians, Italian-Americans, Michael Parenti, religious acculturation, Nicholas Russo, Melford Spiro, structural assimilation
achievement, 150, 151, 152. *See also* Italians, Italian-Americans, Jews, Joseph Lopreato, Bernard Rosen, social class, Fred Strodtbeck
achievement: orientation, 152. *See also* Bernard Rosen
Adorno, T. W., 159
age, 57, 149, 156. *See also* demographic, demographic variables,

immigration, Italians, Italian-Americans
Agger, Robert, 37. *See also* alienation, political cynicism, political efficacy
Aho, William, 156. *See also* class, Italians, Italian-Americans, overachievers, socioeconomic status, social mobility, social class
Aike, M., 36. *See also* alienation, anomie
Albrecht-Carrie, René, 137. *See also* Catholic Church, church, communal tradition, Holy Roman Empire, Italy
alienation, 15, 28–40, 190–91; definition, 28–29; causes and manifestations, 28–29, 31–40. *See also* J. C. Abegglen, Joel Aberbach, Gilbert Abscarian, Robert Agger, M. Aiken, Gabriel Almond, anomie, apathy, C. C. Bowman, Daniel Bell, Robert Blauner, Albert Cohen, Dwight Dean, disaffection, Emile Durkheim, Sebastian de Grazia, educational attainment, estrangement, exclusion, Ada Finfiter, Erich Fromm, T. M. Furst,

237

Christian Democratic Party, 140, 149. *See also* Catholic Church, Italy, Italian politics

church, 137, 138–40, 165. *See also* Catholics, René Albrecht-Carrie, Italy, Italians, Italian-Americans

church-state relations, 139. *See also* Church, Italy, J. C. Jemolo

cinema, 52, 191. *See also* Italians, Italy, Italian-Americans

City College, 184. *See also* Mario Procaccino

civic assimilation, 91. *See also* acculturation, assimilation, behavior receptional assimilation, attitude receptional assimilation, structural assimilation, marital assimilation

class, 18, 27, 75–77. *See also* class identification, ideological identification, Italy, social class

class identification, 214. *See also* class, ideological identification, Italy, social class

class system, 75–77, 151–52. *See also* class, Italy, social class

cleavages, 130, 131, 132. *See also* Laurence Hazelrigg, religion

Cleveland, 16

Clifton, 48. *See also* New Jersey

Cohen, Albert, 32. *See also* alienation, anomie

Columbia Broadcasting Company, 15. *See also* mayoralty campaign, 1969

communal tradition, 135. *See also* René Albrecht-Carrie, Italy

community, 21, 43–49, 50–71, 191. *See also* R. Breton, enclave, Amatai Etzioni, Milton Gordon, ethnic subsociety, Italians, Italian-Americans, neighborhood

Connecticut, 18, 46, 48. *See also* New Haven

conservative, 15, 131, 132, 198. *See also* ideological, identification, Italian-Americans

Contadini, 75–76. *See also* Italy, peasants

control group, 16, 48. *See also* Anglo-Saxons, Protestants, Wasps

Converse, Philip. *See also* Angus Campbell, ethnic voting, voting

core society, 22, 206–9. *See also* Anglo-Saxons, Protestants, Wasps

Cornwell, Elmer, 127. *See also* ethnic voting, party identification, voting

Covello, Leonard, 78, 79, 80, 82. *See also* education, Italians, Italian-Americans, social system, Italy

Crespi, Leo, 28. *See also* methodology

cultural assimilation, 21. *See also* acculturation, assimilation, civic assimilation, behavior receptional, assimilation, attitude-receptional assimilation, structural assimilation, marital assimilation

cultural pluralism, 90. *See also* assimilation, melting pot

culture goals. *See* anomie, Thomas Merton

cynicism, 37, 177. *See also* Robert Agger, Edgar Litt, political cynicism

Dahl, Robert, 18, 19. *See also* political alienation

Darroch, Gordon A., 67. *See also* ethnicity, ethnic group

data collection, 24–28. *See also* methodology, recording data

day laborers, 75–76. *See also* Italy

Dean, Dwight, 36. *See also* alienation, anomie

decision-making, 21, 72–86. *See also* American political system, family, Italian-Americans

declared destination, 51. *See also* immigration

de Grazia, Sebastian, 31–32. *See also* alienation, anomie

dehumanization, 30. *See also* Daniel Bell

De Masi, Domenico, 53

Democratic Party, 37, 118, 127, 186–88, 203–5; party identification, 23,